FREE TO FAIL

Russ Parker was born in Birkenhead and, since becoming a Christian in 1966, has exercised a wide-ranging ministry in both Baptist and Anglican churches. He has been co-Tutor in Pastoral Counselling at St John's College, Nottingham, and his published works include *Healing Dreams* (SPCK 1988), and *The Occult: Deliverance from Evil* (IVP 1989). He is now a Field Officer for the Acorn Christian Healing Trust, and is married and lives in Leicestershire.

D1412931

FREE TO FAIL

RUSS PARKER

TRi△NGLE

First published 1992
Triangle
SPCK
Holy Trinity Church
Marylebone Road
London NW1 4DU

British Library Cataloguing in Publication Data
A catalogue record for this book is available from the
British Library.

ISBN 0–281–04527–2

Typeset by Inforum Typesetting, Portsmouth
Printed and bound in Great Britain by
BPCC Hazells Ltd
Member of BPCC Ltd

CONTENTS

ACKNOWLEDGEMENTS

I would like to thank everyone who has helped me to write this book, who has offered me their criticisms and ideas as well as personal experiences. In particular I think of my wife Carole who has had to listen to all my moans and rages when things have gone wrong for me and I have not had enough faith or patience to wait upon God. I would like to thank all the members of the Rhino Club which includes Eric Delve, our beloved secretary or 'charger', Michael Mitton, J. John, Frs Ian Petit and Pat Lynch, Adrian Plass and Stewart Henderson, dear friends and brothers in Christ with whom I am comfortable to own my many failures. Finally, I would like to thank Heather who has typed my words into some sense even if towards the end I was handing her the script, sheet by sheet.

RP

INTRODUCTION

I started to write this book in 1989 but could not put down one single word for over a year as I was very ill with a serious liver complaint. On Palm Sunday that year my whole ministry came to a sudden halt as I stood in the pulpit of my church and found that I could not think of one word to say. I felt very faint and still do not fully know how I managed to complete the communion service. The following day I began to bleed quite badly and had to go to bed. What followed was almost a year of confinement and inactivity.

I was in and out of hospital a few times during various 'scares' but nothing substantial was ever discovered apart from the rather sweeping diagnosis, that I was suffering from some form of viral debility. So I lay in the vicarage trying to relax, but I could not shut out the sounds of work going on around me and so I eventually decided to go away to convalesce.

Just before I left I had quite a lot of visitors who wanted to know what was going on and to help me if they could. A variety of reasons were put forward for my illness happening at this time; it was demonic attack – my book on the occult and deliverance ministry had just been published. I am sure there is some truth in this as I look back now. However, my friends prayed over me and rebuked whatever spirits were attacking me and commanded deliverance and healing. I remained ill and virtually unable to walk. I began to wonder if I was doubting God and not believing enough for my release. Needless to say, I felt guilty for not recovering. I felt a failure in succumbing to illness, and in not being able to do my work.

Another time I was visited by a number of Pentecostal ministers which included a pastor from New Zealand. As he prayed for me he said that my illness was a result of a curse put on me by a disgruntled member of my church. Consequently he prayed that God would remove the curse and punish the offender. I felt just as ill afterwards but began to wonder who the offender in my church was. Eventually I gave up. There were less provocative suggestions from others, such as that my illness had been sent because I had been overworking and this was God's way of stopping me; or that I was ill because I had not prayed enough for healing at an earlier time when I had had early warnings that something was wrong with me.

The point I am trying to make is that I really had no idea what caused my illness and collapse but that I was put under more pressure by well-meaning friends who felt they had the right understanding of my failure in health. A turning point came when I told a friend that I could not agree with his opinion of what lay behind my illness. I was grateful for his care of me but I just wanted to put aside trying to live up to his diagnosis because it was not my conviction. He was a little taken aback but accepted what I said. The relief I felt was enormous! Far too often we are like King Saul who tried to put his own armour on to David, with the result that David couldn't fight his own battles (1 Sam. 17.38–39). One of the ways in which we free others to handle their own failure appropriately is to stop expecting them to live up to our explanations of the reasons for their failure.

I have learned to accept that not every failure is explained and that 'not knowing why' is something we have to live with. The important thing is to walk with God and stay open to him. Therefore the purpose of this book is to explore our experience of failure as Christians and to see some of the ways God has called us to handle this. The ultimate model for us is Jesus, who had his failures just like the rest of us. This is not an attempt to explain why things go wrong, although we can readily appreciate what some people have gained through their times of loss. Some who suffer physically have testified to discovering anew how to receive the love of God; others whose businesses have collapsed point out that such was the time when they were freed to serve God in a new way. Yet it is not so easy to find a satisfying reason for the person whose marriage has ended in the divorce courts and who feels guilty because their dreams have been dashed. Or to offer an acceptable purpose for the broken health and disillusionment of the missionary who returns home exhausted and with nothing to show for his or her labours.

Whatever our experience of failure there are no easy answers to heal our hurts. Therefore it is the scope of this book to explore some of the pressures to succeed among Christians, and to see if there is a gospel which embraces and to some degree, makes sense of failure.

1 *WINNERS AND LOSERS*

I'd practised looking stunned again,
I'd had another gin,
My agent and my sweetheart
Were sure that I would win.
But when they read the name out – oh, the swine!
Four thousand had made sure it wasn't mine.

Nobody gave me an Oscar,
Nobody called me a star,
Nobody yelled or felt compelled
To drag me to the bar.

Some hoped it would be Dustin's night,
Some felt so close to Glenn,
They'd even changed their lipstick
(And that was just the men).
And then the moment came, and there was I,
Trying to smile and wishing I could die.

Nobody gave me an Oscar,
Nobody swooned at my feet,
No mogul swore he knew I'd score
And swell his balance sheet.
Nobody gave me an Oscar –
But I've still got my conceit.

Roger Woddis[1]

It does not take a genius to realise that much of our modern culture is geared to winning, whatever the cost. During the summer of 1989 Japan went through a period of political turmoil as various scandals relating to bribery and corruption rocked the stability and prestige of the ruling Liberal Democrat Party. The allegations were linked to political favours and winning industrial contracts in return for certain 'gifts'. The individuals concerned were former premiers and high-ranking members of the government. The party which had ruled the nation virtually since the end of the Second World War seemed to be in danger of collapsing. For some, the price for losing even led to suicide. Winning had a price but losing was intolerable.

Politics is one of the great arenas where the battle for power is most seriously and publicly fought out. Winning, not policy, is the chief concern. In Britain, the last few years have seen the Labour Party purging itself of leftist influences to become more acceptable to the electorate. The Liberal-Social Democrat Alliance, in a move to improve its political standing, formed itself into a new, crisp party called the Liberal Democrats. In the last year of her premiership, Margaret Thatcher carried out yet another ministerial reshuffle, bringing new and younger faces into the cabinet. This 'winning team' would, she confidently predicted, take the Conservatives to yet another term of Tory successes – and, it was inferred, make her the first prime minister to be elected four times in succession. How ironic that with the fall in her popularity over her European policies and the Poll Tax, she herself was toppled from the leadership a few months later.

Such concern for power and winning is by no means confined to Britain. During the 1988 presidential election race, the Democratic Party sought to overtake George Bush's lead by alleging that his running mate, Senator Dan Quayle, had failed to fight for his country in the Vietnam war by draft dodging and joining the National Guard instead. The contest hotted up as they also highlighted his inability to debate and discuss in public. Both parties were continuing to describe the other as a losing combination even as the people went to the polls. The Democratic Party financed a television commercial entitled, 'Dan Quayle is only a heart-beat away from occupying the White House', which conjured up visions of a country liable to chaos if left in his incapable hands should Mr Bush be too ill to continue in office. The country had something of a scare in 1990 when this supposed nightmare nearly came true, when President Bush had to go into hospital for what turned out to be a minor operation. Such unsavoury behaviour did not matter, it seems, because winning is the name of the game.

Within hours of his miraculous return to office in Moscow after the abortive coup in 1991, Mikhail Gorbachev was fighting for his political life. Owing to the meteoric rise to prominence of his arch-rival Boris Yeltsin, the Premier began to do a complete about face on his beliefs in order to escape falling from office. He resigned the chairmanship of the Soviet Communist Party and almost immediately gave orders to end the seventy-year rule of the very party which gave him his power. Staying in power it seems, was the name of the game.

Staying on top is also a major factor behind the comparatively high standard of living that we, the rich nations, continue to enjoy. As long ago as 1975, John V. Taylor in his excellent book *Enough is Enough*[2] was one of the first Christian writers to challenge the attitudes of the more powerful economic nations towards their Third World neighbours, accusing them of bending the rules to make sure of winning every game in the law of supply and demand. He quoted as an example how the richer nations fix the prices of poorer nations' tea and sugar crops at a lower level than actually required by the vendor. They do this by exercising their bargaining muscle and by monopoly buying of such crops. The poorer nations are obliged to play this losing game if they wish to sell their products in quantity. So while we may rejoice in whatever foreign aid is given to poor nations, the balance is more than tipped in favour of the donor country by such winning tactics in the market place.

Taylor saw behind such economic practices 'the state of mind of a spoilt child, petulantly greedy and ready to kick to bits anything that frustrates its will'.[3] Little has changed since he wrote those words. Christians have, far too simply, expounded the sins of Marxist countries with their atheistic bias and poor human rights record whilst glibly accepting the 'blessings' of a consumerist and capitalist society. Andrew Walker has shown how, as the richer nations exercise a sort of rampant individualism to succeed in a so-called free enterprise system of marketing, they quite forget other nations' needs and interests as they pursue wealth for itself.[4]

Happily, this imbalance is being somewhat redressed as some Christian groups have begun to focus their attention on the needs of their own home front. In Britain, the Scottish Episcopalian Church at its 1988 Edinburgh Conference and the Methodist Church at its 1989 Leicester Conference challenged the government to pay more attention to the high unemployment rate and the deteriorating Health Service. Archbishop George Carey and Cardinal Basil Hume have challenged Conservative policies on education. They have sought to draw attention to the need for the government to be more concerned about the welfare of its own citizens rather than inexorably pursuing a policy of acquiring wealth and prestige. The policies that might be winners in the market place seem to be lost on those in the housing estates and deteriorating inner cities of our land. Such people feel forgotten and ignored. When

4

their frustration explodes in anger, particularly among black communities, it is dismissed as merely vandalism and calculated racist demonstrations. The appalling poverty and living conditions are somehow glossed over. It seems that we are more than able to bask in the sunshine of our successes but have little or no ability to acknowledge or deal with our failures.

The preoccupation with success runs like a thread through every strand of our society. There was consternation at the 1988 Seoul Olympics when it was discovered that the record breaking, gold-medal run of Ben Johnson in the 100 metres was aided by steroid drugs. The euphoria and adulation of the previous day evaporated in a wave of condemnation. He was stripped of his medal, his world record was struck from the books and he was banned from competitive athletics. The winner had been caught cheating and so he was disgraced, perhaps because he had brought the status of winning into disrepute. The opening of the 1987/8 football season in Britain was marked by fierce fighting among the fans at the Scarborough v. Wolves match. It was reported that the fighting was caused by disgruntled Wolves fans who felt frustrated that their team had sunk to the fourth division from the first. They did not know how to cope with their feelings of failure.

A unique reversal of this trend, turning failure into success, was seen during the 1988 Winter Olympics at Calgary. The man who came last in the 90-metre ski-jump was a plasterer from Cheltenham, Eddie 'the Eagle' Edwards. But the very fact that he came last made him into a popular hero. Within weeks he was appearing on the Johnny Carson Show in America alongside Burt Reynolds and on 'Wogan' in Great Britain. He was much sought after to open new shopping complexes and to appear on television quiz shows which featured sports stars, competing with them in games of knowledge. A West German television company wants to make a documentary of his life. All this popular acclaim for a friendly, affable young man who after practising on the dry slopes of his home town, went to Canada and came in last in his event. He even repeated the feat the following year. The popular press glamorised his failure into something that was funny and commended him for at least daring to try to win. The idea caught on with the public precisely because failure in attempting to win is an all-too-familiar experience. Here was someone who could, however briefly, represent us in our own failures. Nobody likes losing but if it can be turned into some kind of merit then it is not so bad. So this likeable and bubbly man from Cheltenham became a sort of hero figure for all who have tried and failed. It all points to the fact that we all need heroes.

Another kind of hero is someone who seemingly comes back from the dead. Such a person is the Welshman, Simon Weston. When HMS *Galahad*, was set ablaze by an exocet missile during the Falklands War of 1983, Simon was horribly burned and needed years of plastic surgery to rebuild his face and body. The emotional scars will take a lot longer to heal. His road to recovery was revealed in a trilogy of films made by the BBC. The final instalment, 'Simon's Triumph' was shown in April 1989 and showed him living in Liverpool and establishing an adventure course to develop the character and qualities of young people living in urban priority areas. It is called Weston Spirit. One could not but admire his openness about his pain and anger in his fight to rebuild his life. His mother said of him, 'He's a much nicer boy than the one who went to war.' Here was a hero for people to admire. He had overcome great odds and still retained his joy of life. He had been knocked down but not out. For so many who have been knocked out by their personal failures, there is a great need to identify with someone who has been down where they have been and yet has won through! Such a victory gives others hope that they too can win. Naturally, for Christians our true hero is Jesus, and we shall examine later in this book his experience of failure and resurrection which brings us true hope and a model for handling our own failure.

If we would know what are the present cultural myths, we must turn to advertising and the media. And the message they proclaim is, 'It is important to be on top'; 'New means better.' No longer is it important to be who I am; it is more important to give the right impression and to keep up appearances. Being successful is equated with being right. Vance Packard illustrated this point a few years ago by outlining how cars were being sold in America:

> Plymouth quoted a happy family, standing before their long, long car, and disclosing proudly, 'We are not wealthy, we just look it.' Dodge, in one of its radio commercials, depicted an admiring man exclaiming excitedly to a Dodge owner, 'Boy, you must be rich to own a car as big as this.' Ford depicted an actress pointing to the Ford's enormous tail lights, and explained that they 'let people behind you know that you are ahead of them'.[5]

Nowadays the British television advertisements show us various makes of cars either racing through forest fires and coming out without so much as the windscreen clouding over; or easily traversing an obstacle course resembling a high-wire trapeze act and landing the driver safely ahead of her rivals who languish in a traffic jam! The appeal of becoming a winner, or being superior, is unmistakable. Even life insurance is now sold in

England not on the advantages offered by its cover but because the company is a winner – just look at how much it has in the bank. One company asks such questions as, 'Who was the second man to climb Mount Everest or to walk on the Moon?' The advert then makes the point that no one remembers who came in second and that is why the viewer should buy their lifecover, in order not to be a nobody. The media have gone one stage further than merely promoting products; they also manipulate to some degree people's perception of acceptable living. We are told we haven't lived until we have tried a certain item; or we are not acceptable and our currency worthless unless we carry a certain chargecard. Television provides us with living experts to inform us of the latest trends in dress, and where to be seen if we want to be known as an achiever, a person on the way up if not already there.

Nowhere was this more typified than in the 'yuppie' (young urban professional) culture of the 1980s. They epitomised the middle-class values of getting and succeeding at all cost. Their 'fear of failure and of not being accepted motivate many in becoming "Xerox" copies of one another'.[6] Stuart Ewen, social critic and historian, wrote in 1988:

> These young professionals – many of whom are employed by the new 'information industries' – scramble to surround themselves with the ever-changing latest in designer clothing, consumer electronics and other commodified symbols of the good life. As they frenetically pursue this semiotic world of objects . . . all connection to society or to social responsibility, is forsworn in favour of individuals' acquisition and display.[7]

Ewen goes on to paint a sad picture of how such people sacrifice their own emotional well-being in search of achieving status by acquisition and success; personal feelings are relegated to the private domain, as they have no mileage in the business world. Such chasing after fantasies produces what Robert Lifton called a sort of 'psychic numbing' to the soul.[8] By implication it seems that giving a voice to compassion and justice may well affect our ability to gain profit and efficiency. As one line of American graffiti expressed it, 'Nice guys don't win.' Michael Korda, a modern guru of winning, has said in his book, *Power! How to get it – How to use it*, that man has come of age and his real religion is success and its god is power. For him, power gives meaning to life. His book unashamedly sets out to show people how to use power for their own advantage; small wonder that it became an international best seller.

Certainly, power has had a fascination for people throughout the ages. Frederick Nietzsche, the German philosopher, wrote that the hunger for power is the essence of our humanity; for him, the will to power was the basic human drive. This was why he was so opposed to Christianity, because its hero died the death of the vanquished. His followers were actually encouraged to share their weaknesses, and for Nietzsche this smacked of an inferior breed of humanity. Power promises to fulfil our innate longing to be known and understood and accepted. So we begin by amassing the symbols of power, the cream of this world's goods, and going further still we collect people by exerting power over them. Cheryl Forbes, in *The Religion of Power*, writes that imposing such power over people brings not only a feeling of self-control and fulfilment to the perpetrator but also a feeling of omnipotence.[9] The old sin of self-idolatry is encouraged by such an exercise of power.

Yet is power in itself an evil thing? Tolkein certainly implied this in his *Lord of the Rings* trilogy, when Gandalf warns Frodo not to use the ring of power if he can help it because it will corrupt him. He then introduces the character Sméagol, who was transformed from Hobbit into the murderer of his friend, and finally ended his days as the wretched, less-than-human thing called Gollum. Anthony Campolo, in *The Power Delusion*, tries to unpack the workings of power in society and shows that it only leads to corruption when the coercive element of power is employed.[10] Certainly Christians believe in and talk about the power of God in their lives; but we really need to examine whether it is power from on high or power to succeed in our own goals in life which really concerns us. As we shall see later on in this book, power for the Christian lies in service, in giving and not getting (Matt. 20.26).

One factor that has brought to the fore this preoccupation with success and power in the twentieth century has been the explosion of the Human Potential movement. This is basically a mixture of philosophies and New Age ideas which promote the gospel that humankind has the power within itself to do anything it imagines or believes. People are encouraged to have confidence in their own inner potential and gifts, and to step out and create new possibilities for themselves. One of the more popular advocates of this movement is Napoleon Hill who appeals to the self-deification of mankind: 'I no longer seek the will of God. What does He want me to do? I say, What do I want to do?'[11] Hill and other expounders of Human Potential ideas basically appeal to innate human energy which is accredited with an almost infallible sense of knowing what is right. To employ this power is to guarantee success in life, according to the heralds of the movement. We should be very concerned when such ideas enter the Christian world. There is more than a hint of this in such books as *The Power of Positive Thinking* in which Norman Vincent Peale writes about prayer as some

10

kind of independent energy source which simply needs to be tapped in order to secure the things we want in life.[12] It seems that any need for the Holy Spirit and divine grace has been superseded by some human energy called 'prayer'. Prayer now becomes a winning formula in the game of successful living.

Yet it is a sad fact of life that there are a lot more casualties than we care to admit. The *Independent* newspaper forecast that by the end of 1989, the number of deaths through AIDS would reach 4,000. By 1991 this number had almost doubled and doctors were reporting that AIDS is now of epidemic proportions in such African countries as Zimbabwe and Kenya. Suicide is now ranked as the eighth major cause of death in the western hemisphere.[13] One of the major reasons for this is that people have lost a reason for living and cannot cope with the collapse of their hopes. Our own national statistics inform us that approximately fifty per cent of all marriages now end in the divorce court within the first ten years. Counselling figures reveal an alarming rise in the number of people suffering from depression. Our society, it seems, knows how to encourage success but has not taught its members how to cope with failed expectations. The question we have to ask ourselves is whether the Church suffers from the same imbalance. Has it got drunk on the spirit of the age in its quest for power experiences and miracle moments? In the next chapter we shall explore the Christian quest for power and how it has responded to its failures.

> Today our cultural norm will say,
> Successful people are here to stay,
> Substantial people have great vision,
> They are men and women of quick decision,
> And are praised to the heights on television.

But success is like a pyramid,
Only a few will make a bid,
To reach the top,
Most will flop,
And fall below,
There to grow
Weary of the great burden
Failure imposes upon them.

Jeff South[14]

2 WE ARE ON THE WINNING SIDE

'Those who fail are those who try the hardest to succeed.' *Paul Tournier*

Ever since the renewal of interest in the person and work of the Holy Spirit began in the 1960s, there have been great moments of blessing but also great heartaches and disappointments. A fresh dynamism and optimism have sprung up within the church, bringing an expectancy of mighty and miraculous happenings. There has been a landslide of books testifying to phenomenal church growth, amazing healings, an outpouring of charismatic gifts, and deliverance from the power of evil spirits. Two important conferences took place in the United Kingdom in 1990, which reflect the growing awareness of the Holy Spirit moving in power. One was at Brighton where approximately three thousand people gathered to learn and experience the power of deliverance ministry: the power of the Holy Spirit to conquer and cast out evil. The other was in London where almost fifteen hundred gathered for a week to meet with a group known as the Kansas City Prophets. Here they were challenged by the presence of prophets proclaiming God's word in intimate detail for individuals, as well as outlining the victories and strategies that God is about to implement in the nation as a whole as he brings in a tremendous revival. Whatever we may wish to think about these events and experiences, they do none the less have a great impact upon people's faith, and as a consequence increase expectancy that God is about to do great things for them.

Kevin Springer has described the last decades of the twentieth century as being the 'third wave' of the Holy Spirit in power. The thought behind this is that the first wave happened on the day of Pentecost, the second came with the era of the charismatic renewal in the main line denominations. The third (and possibly the last) wave is that of today, with the advent of signs and wonders in ministry.[1] Who has not heard of the tremendous healings and deliverances which have accompanied the 'calling down of the Holy Spirit' upon the congregation by such leaders as John Wimber? However, Wimber would be the first to agree that when we call upon the Holy Spirit to fall upon us we may be asking for more than we bargained for! Indeed, such invitations to the Holy Spirit have been spoken about for some time. Consider the following by no less a churchman than Archbishop William Temple:

When we pray 'Come, Holy Ghost, our souls inspire', we had better know what we are about. He will not carry us to easy triumphs and gratifying successes; more probably He will set us some task for God in the full intention that we shall fail, so that others, learning wisdom by our failure, may carry the good cause forward. He may take us through loneliness, desertion by friends, apparent desertion even by God; that was the way Christ went to the Father . . . For if we invoke Him, it must be to help us in doing God's will, not ours. We cannot call upon the Creator Spirit . . . in order to use omnipotence for the supply of our futile pleasures or the success of our futile plans. If we invoke Him, we must be ready for the glorious pain of being caught by His power out of our petty orbit into the eternal purposes of the Almighty, in whose onward sweep our lives are as a speck of dust. The soul that is filled with the Spirit must have become purged of all pride or love of ease, all self-complacence and self-reliance; but the soul has found the only real dignity, the only lasting joy. Come then, Great Spirit, come. Convict the world; and convict my timid soul.[2]

Temple reminds us that the Holy Spirit does not always bring us into places which we would have liked or expected. There are many Christians for whom the story has been quite different from being on the crest of a wave. There have been denied hopes, splits in churches, an absence of power and great feelings of being ineffectual in service. They have prayed for blessing and power as much as anyone else, but for them it has not happened. Our immediate response is to ask them where they went wrong in their lives, so that we can help them 'get it right' and so find power.

I remember a girl of eighteen coming to talk with me some years ago when I had preached a sermon on the power of prayer. She told me very bluntly that the things I had been suggesting simply did not work! I was flustered, and scrambled around inside my mind for something to say which would make me look good. I asked her the usual things which make people feel uncomfortable. Was she reading her Bible regularly and praying every day? She said 'Yes'. So in an endeavour to extricate myself from her challenge I looked at her seriously and asked her if there was any unconfessed sin in her life which was preventing her from praying properly. She said that as far as she knew there was no such problem at the moment. By now I was getting angry, because I felt that my credentials were under attack and I feared that I would lose status in the eyes of others. I am not proud of my reactions because it became very obvious that I was more concerned about my reputation than with helping this girl to develop her prayer life.

Perhaps we need to remind ourselves that because some things do not work out the way we had hoped, it does not mean that there is something wrong about us or that our faith is lacking in some way.

Of course, it is perfectly legitimate to expect God to be at work in the church, as indeed the Acts of the Apostles bears witness. There were days when thousands were converted; moments of sheer power when people were freed from physical illness and others were brought back from the dead. There were encounters with angels and miraculous escapes from prison and certain death. Yet we do need to realise that we are reading selective history, and that there were also days of failure and persecution when the church seemed to be in derision and retreat. Our problems begin when we see only the days of power and glory and expect this to be our daily diet.

Tom Smail, in *The Giving Gift* introduces another aspect of our difficulty in balancing a right understanding of power with failure. He reminds us that, even though an outpouring of the Holy Spirit in renewal and revival contains the supernatural activity of the Holy Spirit, it also has the upsurging of human exclusiveness, arrogance, disregard for the truth and hunger for power that can frustrate and even threaten to neutralise what the Spirit is doing.[3] He likens this to the Corinthian church, where amidst much that spoke of the Spirit there was mixed much that spoke of human immaturity and sinfulness. I suspect that this is why we can divert our encounter with the Spirit in power into a preoccupation with success and power. The power of love can all too easily be diverted into the love of power! Let us examine, then, some of the influences by which we may become obsessed with power and unable to live with failure.

It was J.B. Phillips in his paraphrased New Testament who translated St Paul's words as: 'Do not let the world squeeze you into its own mould.'[4] This is always a tension for the church which seeks to communicate its message effectively to the society in which it lives. On the one hand we cannot be such purists that we restrict ourselves and the gospel to a sort of Indian reservation of our own making (to use Os. Guiness's analogy),[5] nor on the other do we indiscriminately use secular standards and strategies. Jesus exhorted his disciples to be wise in the ways of the world, but he condemned the wholesale adoption of its standards. In the parable of the steward who is commended by his master for shrewd business deals, Jesus actually delivers the punch line that though we may reap success through sharp business practices we shall not be trusted with handling the business of God's kingdom.[6]

Andrew Walker in his book *Enemy Territory* gives a graphic account of the church both seeking to use secular forms of communication and competition, while at the same time becoming captive to the spirit of the age. He refers to the religious sect in North America which renounces humanism when it threatens the fundamental truths of God's revelation of himself in the sacred Scripture, yet embraces the worldliness and materialism of advanced industrialism and even declares it good![7] It seems that the church considers itself rather on the scale of a large business conglomerate which has to compete in the market place in order to sell its product. John White questions whether our wholesale adoption of secular technology has not catapulted the church into a love of self where the emphasis has been placed on the Christian super-personality rather than on the gospel of our Lord Jesus Christ.[8] Once we have decided to compete in the market place, we need effective advertising and the raising of money to keep the machinery and the medium afloat. Especially with regard to television, White shows how the church has had to adopt the entertainment model in order to attract 'customers'. Christian celebrities are presented in order to show that the gospel has meaning. Athletes share how they are trusting Jesus to help them to excel and win. One reason for the popularity of the film *Chariots of Fire* was the image of the Christian runner, Eric Liddell, claiming (in the words of the script writer Colin Welland), that the power to win comes from within. It showed that his faith in God helped him to be a winner. Such a message appeals to millions who long to be winners themselves. Yet it is a salutory reminder that Jesus came not to win but to save.

Now it must be said that the church does need to reach out to its community with the message of the gospel; and to do so it needs to be conversant with prevailing trends and attitudes. However, this does not necessarily mean that we have to go about it as if we are exercising a take-over bid of a company. Jesus made it quite clear that we would receive tribulation within the world, and he also warned about the dangers of competing with the world in order to win its praise (cf. Matt. 6.1–4). Therefore, in this decade when evangelism and revival are very much upon the agenda, we need to be sure that our methods as well as our objectives conform to the Gospel mandate and not to the desire to be successful in the world and to be recognised as such. That is why it is not helpful, as happens in some circles, to talk about 'taking the city for the King' or 'winning the country for Jesus'. This fails to take into account that it is persons whom we are seeking to reach and not structures. Hence Walker points out that the commitment to compete in the market place has been at the expense of 'realising' the kingdom of God amongst us, in individual and church alike. Another casualty of this obsession, he claims, is that the church has in fact lost such a bid and in effect has itself been reduced to a consumer product. 'Christianity is now on "special offer" in multiform shapes and sizes. Competing in the open market with other religions and with atheistic philosophies, there is a broad choice of "real" and "best" Christianities for anyone who wants to buy.'[9] So we have come to a place where secular man and woman regard Christian worship and commitment as a hobby or interest to be put alongside golf or old-time dancing. Far from competing from within the secular structures, the Church should be challenging its world to conform to God's standards. It needs to recover its prophetic challenge to society, and from such a place of proclamation seek to make disciples of Jesus Christ, whatever the personal cost it may have to suffer. As John V. Taylor says, the Church has for too long been seduced into thinking of itself as an institution alongside other institutions.[10] By doing so it has become embroiled in securing its own power structure within an overall secular power structure. Yet in essence the Church is a movement, and as such it is mobile and flexible enough to minister to its society rather than compete with it.

Selfism: The Secular Faith of the Age

One of the contributors to the market-place practices of successful expansionism and power is the philosophy of self. This is a belief in the power of human capability to achieve success against all odds. Coupled with this is the message that success is within the normal capabilities of any hard worker. According to Richard Quebedeaux, this kind of new thought coupled with a restructured evangelicalism produces the selfist theology of such people as Norman Vincent Peale and

Robert Schuller.[11] The values of human achievement and self-worth become central to this doctrine, and so we are encouraged to reach for the skies because we can be a success if we only try.

Consider for example the following extracts from the works of Robert Schuller which illustrate this new gospel of success:

> Jesus knew his worth, his success fed his self-esteem. And he bore the cross to sanctify your self-esteem. The cross will sanctify the ego trip.[12]

> I don't think anything has been done in the name of Christ . . . that has proven more destructive to the human personality, and hence counterproductive to the evangelism enterprise, than the often crude, uncouth and unchristian strategy of attempting to make people aware of their lost and sinful condition.[13]

Here is a Christ who feeds our esteem rather than forgives our sins. Such an over-emphasis on our worth in God's eyes has undoubtedly focused our attentions too much upon the need to succeed in order to gain esteem in our own eyes and in the eyes of our peers. This breeds competitiveness and the comradeship of the achievers, and not the fellowship of the forgiven. It is a gospel for the powerful, not for the weak and broken of the world. There is a scene in the film version of Paul Gallico's novel, *The Poseidon Affair*, where a stricken ship is sinking and two clergymen find themselves responding to the panic among the passengers. One is young and determined, and gathers around him a group of strong people who make a bid to escape from the ship. Before leaving, he notices the older clergyman sitting down with the depressed passengers who have obviously given up all hope of getting out. 'Why don't you save yourself and join us?' he asks. 'Don't give in to weakness like the rest of these people.' The older priest replies, 'You only have a gospel for the strong. Where is your good news for the weak? I will stay here with the hopeless, at least they will know that they have not been abandoned. Someone has got to stay here and support the weak.'

Douglas Frank, in his revealing book *Less Than Conquerors*, outlines a number of evangelical movements at the turn of the century in the United States which advocated a gospel for the strong as an antidote to the failure of the church to remain at the centre of the nation's life and politics. Amongst those he examines he mentions the evangelicalism of Billy Sunday and the Victorious Life movements. Billy Sunday put at the heart of his message an appeal to Americans to be really strong and manly and so become Christians.[14] This was the new morality for those who recognised their own importance and power. Sunday spoke of the world's weak morality and Christ's manly morality for those who have the courage to be brave and adventurous. 'Sunday believed that through moral exertion they would once again – and deservedly – be at the helm of an earthly kingdom, and all would be well.'[15] What at first glance seems to be a challenge to fulfilment is seen to be nothing more than a yearning for power and prestige within the world.

Frank also states that another form of inability to handle failure lies at the root of preoccupation with holiness and perfection. The Holiness movements recognised that religion had lost the battle for predominance in secular or public life and so transferred their focus to winning the battle within and that of conquering sin in the human heart by the predominance of Christian holiness. In contrast to regaining the centre of secular life, the Holiness movements offered an inner triumph over the true reason for failure, our sin. The triumph of rigorous faith is internalised and so a private victory is won over the world. Our experience of holiness takes us into a personal world of the Spirit which cannot be invaded by our fallen society. As a student at Bible college I came across a pamphlet entitled, *Purity before Power*, which suggested that this power in and over life was only obtainable after experiencing a sanctification of the whole of one's life. Purity thus sometimes looked like a carrot to gain power and therefore status in the eyes of others. It is not the purpose of this book to disparage personal morality and holiness of life, but we do need to be careful about our motivation. It is so difficult sometimes to separate a genuine and wholesome belief from the all-pervading temptation to have an affair with power.

This gospel for the strong created a climate of expectancy amongst Christians; it encouraged its adherents to jump into the maelstrom of life and to view any success achieved as a sign of God's favour. This comes very close to the belief typical of the Old Testament period. The catch, though, was that any failure meant abandonment by God, or temporary disfavour at the very least. The result of this kind of high-pressure living by faith was nervous exhaustion or elation, depending upon whether we failed or succeeded. There are two particular areas we need to examine which have been influenced to some degree by this climate of expectancy.

EVANGELICAL CERTAINTIES
As an evangelical I believe, amongst other things, in the God who has and does act decisively in people's lives for their salvation. I also uphold the Bible as God's written self-revelation, displaying his purposes and his principles. However, one of the by-products of these beliefs is a water-tight theology with no room for gaps. What this means is that every event has to have a place

in a neat and precise theological pyramid. On this view, failure becomes something which God has foreseen and incorporates into his scheme of teaching us some lesson. It gives rise to such clichés as, 'God will not lead you where he cannot keep you.' Yet sometimes it is very hard to glean a lesson from the mental breakdown of ministers who crack under pressure, or from mourning parents who witness the senseless slaughter of their children as at Aberfan in the 1960s or in the drought-ridden Ethiopia of today. Such difficulties in handling failure have less to do with a belief in a sovereign God than with the inability to live with mystery and mess.

Another product of our certainties is preoccupation with defending God from all criticisms. I have already mentioned my problem in talking with a young girl who thought that prayer had no power. But if I am to be totally honest, not only was my prestige under threat but I felt insecure with my certainties. If in fact God did not answer prayer in the way I had preached, then there was the doubt that perhaps I had put my faith in some-one who could not fulfil my expectations. So my haste to defend myself was bound up with the necessity to defend God, because he must not be seen to fail either! I realise that it is ludicrous to try to defend God, who is capable of looking after himself! We do it because we feel our security is being threatened. What a challenge to realise that the Son of God stripped himself of the securities of heaven and lay open and exposed upon the cross for our forgiveness! As we shall explore in a later chapter, the cross also teaches us about God's failure in Christ which is tasted to the full, in order that a way forward in life may be opened.

PARANOIA AND PENTECOST

I remember listening to a friend who was a minister of a major denominational church. He was sharing his feelings of frustration because his church was not growing fast enough. It had come into an experience of charismatic renewal, and the worship had now become a mixture of liturgy and choruses with open prayer and the ministry of healing. However, there were a number of people within his church who felt that some of the more traditional forms of worship were being swept aside, and such criticisms were occupying a lot of the minister's time and attention. Consequently he felt that the momentum of renewal had slowed down. However, it was not this which really preyed upon his mind, but the fact that an evangelical church which was not charismatic, had recently built a 'superbowl'-sized church in his neighbourhood with a seating capacity of two thousand, whereas his church only seated just over two hundred. Therefore he was channelling all his energies into a programme of demolishing his existing church buildings in order to build a bigger church than the evangelicals. 'After all,' said the minister, 'we are the ones who have been filled with the Spirit and so we must have more to show for it!'

I do not want to give the impression that I equate charismatic renewal with a preoccupation with bigness, but I do want to signal the danger of being preoccupied with eventfulness. Because spiritual renewal is an opening to the presence of the Spirit in power, there can be an all-too-quick conclusion that the absence of powerful moments with the Spirit, such as healings, prophecies and deliverances, means that the Spirit of God is not amongst us. Signs and wonders are, after all, testimonies to the presence of the Kingdom and not to the prowess of the Kingdom's disciples. There has in fact been a long history among Christians of using our experiences of power as a justification for our particular cause or belief. John Wesley, for example, justified his anti-Calvinist stance by the manifestations at his meetings. He mentions in his journal an occasion when he cried out to God to affirm the truth of his preaching, and in response a number of people began to fall to the ground as if struck by thunder.[16] It must be said that this was a time of great confrontation and rivalry within the revival movements of the day, and that Wesley was appealing to events of power to substantiate his ministry. He claimed to be in the right because the Holy Spirit was moving in power in his meetings. Yet what a fatal assumption to make. Even Jesus said to some who had prophesied or healed or cast our demons in his name, 'Depart from me, I never knew you!' (Matt. 7.21–23).

So we recognise a possible flaw within our experience of Pentecost – to use our experience of the eventful to justify our ministry. This is, of course, an indication of our innate insecurity, which is properly conquered in our daily walk with God and not in the moments of power in which we share.

Another possible problem with Pentecost is simply when the power is not there and the great events do not happen. This is the moment when paranoia grips the heart. We begin to imagine that perhaps God is blocking our way forward until we learn a lesson, and then he will bless us to our heart's content. Or perhaps we have failed to grasp some basic truth somewhere, and if only we look long and hard and listen to those who have achieved the goals for which we ourselves long, then we will be given space to move out of the spiritual poverty trap. Yet this can become a subtle form of idolatry as we seek to clone our spiritual lives upon those whom we regard as successes. I note with respect the words of John Wimber, who says that he sailed all too lightly into the area of healing in the power of the Spirit, and did not see any healing at all for a year. He also says, however, that during this time he personally learned integrity of heart, and then gradually a healing ministry followed. Perhaps this is a way forward in our discussion: we need to learn integrity in our walk in the Spirit of Pentecost. In our desire for eventfulness we all too often try to reproduce in our world the ministry of some other. We need to maintain our genuineness in this struggle to know God in his power and in his powerlessness. We are too easily impressed with the mighty moments of meaning that for us speak more eloquently of the Spirit of God at work. Consider these words of Henri Nouwen:

> Somehow I keep expecting loud and impressive events to convince me and others of God's saving power; but over and over again I am reminded that spectacles, power plays and events are the ways of the world. Our temptation is to be distracted by them. When I have no eyes for the sweet signs of God's presence – the smile of a baby, the carefree play of children, the words of encouragement and gestures of love offered by friends – I will always remain tempted to despair. The small children of Bethlehem, the unknown young man of Nazareth, the rejected preacher, the naked man on the cross, *he* asks for my full attention.[17]

Renewal is a journey into wholeness in Christ and not just an explosion of power. Therefore the Spirit will want to show us Calvary and our sinfulness and also Pentecost and God's power of love.

One of the more meaningful encounters with the Spirit, for me, happened some years ago when my wife and I were expecting our first child. At that time we were involved in a small prayer group which was beginning to step out in fellowship and spiritual gifts. When one of the leading and more vocal members of this group heard of our expectation, he came around to congratulate us. Before parting we prayed together, and Tom prayed and 'prophesied' over me – my wife was absent at the time.

His prophecy consisted of something like the following: 'I say to you, my child, that the baby in your wife's womb is a boy and he will grow up to be a mighty prophet in the land and serve the Lord in power and love.' You can imagine how pleased I was to think that my son, yet to be born, would be someone whom God would use for his purposes! However, a couple of months later we lost the child in what is known as a spontaneous abortion. What had happened to us? What was God playing at? What about those promises and prophecies? We were devastated and numbed over the whole event. Shortly afterwards there came a knock at the door of our flat and it was Tom. Though he is extremely large in height and weight he looked sheepish and small. All he could say was, 'I'm sorry. I feel such a fraud, please forgive me for what I said.' At that moment my heart melted and I was able to let go of some of my grief and, most remarkable of all, not only did my estimation of Tom's experience of the Spirit go up, but so did my awareness of the Spirit's renewing power. Renewal is the grace to say 'I got it wrong.'

In the next chapter we shall examine some of the doctrines that have emerged from a distorted view of evangelical certainties and charismatic expectancies. However, before doing this we need to conclude this chapter by saying something about the place of spiritual power in the Christian life.

Committed to Power

Any cursory reading of the New Testament will tell us that as Christians and the children of God we are to share in the power of Christ. Consider the following prayer from the pen of the apostle Paul:

> For this reason, because I have heard of your faith in the Lord Jesus and your love towards all the saints, I

do not cease to give thanks for you, remembering you
in my prayers . . . that you may know what is the
hope to which he has called you, what are the riches
of his glorious inheritance in the saints, and what is
the immeasurable greatness of his power in us who
believe (Eph. 1.15–19RSV).

Added to this example are others such as the commis-
sioning of the disciples to go out and proclaim the gospel of the Kingdom in power and authority (Luke 9.1);
Paul in his personal quest longs for the power of
Christ's resurrection to be manifested in his life (Phil.
3.10); and Jesus tells his disciples at their final meeting
before his ascension that they are to wait in Jerusalem
until they receive the Holy Spirit and power (Luke
24.49). Therefore a Christian is to live in the power of
God's spirit.

Where we need to be careful is in deciding to what
ends the power is to be used. While it is true that we
have the power and authority in Jesus's name to cast out
demons and break down the strongholds of evil in
people's lives and minds, we do not have the power to
avoid failure or suffering. Far too often we have allowed
our experience of God's power to tempt us into a kind
of empty triumphalism, where we blot out the pain of
failure with a promise of lessons soon to be learned
which will make all things well. Valerie Lesniak calls this
the 'saccharine spirituality syndrome'.[18] A couple of
years ago a preacher was given a genuine gift of healing
as he prayed for someone in his church. However, from
that moment on he became convinced that everyone he
now prayed for must be completely healed, and that
nothing less would be acceptable. While this may at first
glance seem a commendable faith, it also caused devastating problems for him and for some of the people he
tried to help. In particular there was a young woman

dying of bone cancer and he regularly prayed for her healing. As her condition worsened he began to believe that it
was a test from God, that if he persevered he would pass
the test and God would eventually heal the woman. When
finally the woman died, he was devastated and wondered
if he had prayed enough, or if the Devil had somehow
crept in at the last minute. Far from appreciating that for
the Christian death is the greatest healing we can experience, he became morose and lost sight of God, and his
faith suffered greatly. He had allowed his experience of
healing power to become obsessional and had forgotten
that all healing belongs to God and that it is up to him
what he does in answer to our prayers. One moment of
power to heal is not a promise that there will be no more
suffering or failure in the world.

So, while we experience the power of God, we do not
have power in order to be powerful people. So often
God's power is revealed in weakness. David Prior
points out how the incarnation of the King of the Jews
as a new-born baby reveals the power of God in the
helplessness of the child.[19] He goes on to ask, 'Does the
baby of Bethlehem not reveal God rather than obscure
him?'[20] Helpless, yet he commands the attention of the
Magi and the shepherds as well as the fear and hostility
of Herod. Helpless, yet he is the focus for the power of
God at work amongst men. St Paul eventually learned
this lesson when he exchanged the clamour for visions
for the weakness that allowed God's power to flow
through him to others (2 Cor. 12.9–10).

Let us look at how this power of God is modelled in
the life of Jesus and the early disciples.

Power to serve
'For the Son of Man also came not to be served but
to serve, and to give his life as a ransom for many.'
(Mark 10.45RSV)

When Jesus summed up his life to his friends it was in terms of a servant. This was a total departure from the normal concept of power and Jesus underlined this. Godly power was to be used to give, and not to take from others. Jesus also linked power with sacrifice and vulnerability; his life was to be given as a ransom. This is an uncomfortable association for the powerful, because secular society links power with strength. Jesus links power with service. It was this which threatened the Pharisees who saw in Jesus' way of life the supreme threat to their power base in the community.

Matthew, when narrating the entrance of Jesus into Jerusalem on a donkey, described him as being humble and yet also an overcoming king (Matt. 21.1–5). Yet this was an apt description for one who would channel God's power, because the Greek word for humility here (*praus*) means power in harness. If we want to be people through whom God is at work, then we must learn to humble ourselves and serve. Such service will take us all the way to the cross, as it did for Jesus: and that cross will break us, but it will transform us. There are far too many Christians today who long for the power of God but who cannot come to terms with Calvary moments. The old cross spoke of suffering and sacrifice but, in the words of A.W. Tozer, 'The new cross does not slay the sinner, it redirects him. It gears him into a new, cleaner and jollier way of living and saves his self-respect.'[21]

Power to save

'I am not ashamed of the gospel: it is the power of God for salvation to everyone who has faith.' (Romans 1.16rsv)

Spiritual power is also to do with the stripping down of our strengths and being made aware of our need for God. Therefore, far from being a people who cover over our failures and faults with a show of power, we are to be those who continually know our need of grace and salvation. It is precisely for this reason that we are enabled to conquer the powers of darkness in the name of Jesus. We know the power of God for us who believe, because it has brought us to repentance, and therefore deliverance from the kingdom of darkness (Col. 1.13). Because we have come under God's authority we now walk in the awareness of our continual need of his saving presence within.

Resurrection power

'For His sake I have suffered the loss of all things and count them as refuse, in order that I might gain Christ and be found in him . . . that I may know him, and the power of his resurrection, and may share his sufferings, becoming like him in his death.' (Philippians 3.8–10 RSV)

Paul is very clear that resurrection power is wrapped up in tasting the death of Christ. As with Jesus, therefore, spiritual power has nothing to do with actually making a bid for power, but with choosing to suffer loss in order that God's power may bring release and healing in others. Cheryl Forbes points out that today's Christians down-play sacrifice and service, commitment and discipline. Now the popular call is to do your own thing or fulfil your gifts of power.[22] Resurrection power is knowing how to die to the glamour of a powerful self in order that the Christ-like life may grow and be formed in us.

Power of forgiveness

'As the Father has sent me, even so I send you.' And when he had said this, he breathed on them, and said to them, 'Receive the Holy Spirit. If you forgive the sins of any, they are forgiven; if you retain the sins of any, they are retained.' (John 20.21–23 RSV)

In this foretaste of the Holy Spirit's power, how very different it feels to that on the day of Pentecost. Both experiences occur in an upper room but on this occasion it is peace which characterises the giving of the Spirit. One of the familiar themes I heard at Bible College in the late 1960s was that the Holy Spirit comes to give us power for service. How very true this is. However, the service which we cannot afford to withhold is that of forgiveness. I often think that there is more evidence of the Spirit's power at work in the heart when it learns to let go of what it holds against another and releases this in Jesus' name, than in the power which heals a broken body or which gives a word of prophecy. The secular image of power is of what it gains over another and acquires in assets for itself. Spiritual power is demonstrated in what it can let go of for the benefit of another. Forgiveness is that ministry by which whatever is held against a person is now removed and the other person is given space to grow and find freedom. This is true of Christ and Calvary, for whoever would find his or her way to the cross finds a God who has stretched out his arms for us and is saying, 'Look! To all who come to this place, I hold nothing against them. Go free in my name.'

It is quite remarkable that in the words of Jesus spoken just after he received the fullness of the Spirit and power, he talked of healing and releasing as a ministry of forgiveness: 'The Spirit of the Lord is upon me, because he has anointed me to preach good news to the poor. He has sent me to proclaim release (forgiveness) to the captives (unforgiven), and recovering of sight to the blind, to set at liberty those who are oppressed.' (Luke 4.18–19RSV. Words in brackets are mine.)

Victorious power
'Then one of the elders said to me, "Weep not; for

the Lion of the tribe of Judah, the Root of David, has conquered, so that he can open the scroll and its seven seals.'' And between the throne and the four living creatures among the elders, I saw a Lamb standing, as though it had been slain . . .' (Revelation 5.5–6 RSV)

I am indebted to David Prior who points out that as the apostle John gazes through into eternity and foresees the almighty and triumphing power of God, what he actually sees is a Lamb.[23] While there have been references to the roaring Lion of Judah, at the heart of this conquest is the picture of the sacrificed rather than the victor. Yet it was precisely because of this sacrifice that Jesus was launched into triumph and conquest of his enemies. Prior describes this as the reversing factor of the Second Coming. While we certainly do await the coming of Jesus as King of Kings, he will still carry the stamp of the Lamb of God. The wounds and scars will not be hidden in some kind of cosmetic display of glory. They will be there for all to see, and so glory and sacrifice will be balanced perfectly in the reign of the Lamb upon his throne.

In conclusion therefore, we are to be channels of the power of God, but such power is to enable us to empty ourselves of our pride and self-centredness and focus upon the needs of others. We shall indeed see our mighty times, with signs and wonders, but we are not to think for a moment that we can borrow this power in a bid to make ourselves strong in the eyes of others. This was, after all, the original rebellion that took place in Eden. No matter how exhilarated we will feel as we see God's power at work through us, we must make sure that the praise goes to God, and not be tempted to shun the marks of a sacrificed lamb that will follow in its wake.

3 DOCTRINES OF DISTORTION

'Before long, I gradually became aware something sinister was happening within the renewal movement. The early emphasis on Jesus as Lord and on His endowment of His Church with the power and gifts of the Holy Spirit was shifting, was being obscured. One new teaching after another – each with some new emphasis – vied for top billing. Many of these teachings were based on valid biblical principles, but the principles were being twisted and pushed to excess. People were falling for distorted doctrines, and deception was taking a tremendous toll on some who had started out so well.' *Florence Bulle*[1]

There are some teachings abroad today which are the product of a need for certainty and success in the spiritual life. They convey an absolute guarantee of obtaining the desired goal, be it power in ministry, healing or material blessings. The common denominator of these teachings seems to be triumph – victory over all the adversities and trials of this life. However, upon closer inspection we find that this is not the triumph of the Crucified but the empty triumphalism of an inflated selfism which cannot deliver what it promises.

Such beliefs are presented as a fail-safe opportunity to achieve or overcome. Any failures are simply ascribed to the lack of proper application by the individual. Of course, the danger in such an approach to spiritual growth is that it not only condemns those who do not achieve but implies an idolatrous confidence in our own abilities. At the same time we must not undermine the fact that our God does reign and that he does heal, he does pour out his Spirit in power upon us, and through faith teaches us to be more than conquerors through him. It is when we automatically link conquering with the glitter of success or winning without losses that we arrive at a distortion of belief. Each of the doctrines we shall review has a truth about it, but they are all really an expression of belief that there is no room for failure if we are to be the powerful people of God.

Prosperity Teachings

Among the many missionary and evangelical magazines we read at Bible College there was one from a certain revivalist who offered his readers a 'Pact of Plenty'. What this meant was that if I subscribed to his evangelical ministry around the world, then he and his wife would covenant to pray for me in return. I was promised that, as a result of my commitment and faithfulness, God would reward me with increase and abundance. There followed a number of testimonies from various people who had done this, and they reported such blessings as receiving promotion at work, being able to buy a bigger house or being given enough money to go on a holiday of a lifetime. I can assure you that as a student on a very basic income, I found that such invitations to prosperity appealed more to my greed than to my faith towards God.

The basic thrust of these prosperity teachings is that if we give sacrificially to God, he will in turn ensure that we have blessings in abundance. Some of the more well-known advocates of this doctrine, whose lifestyles seem to demonstrate such faith, are the successful American evangelists Kenneth Hagin and his disciple, Kenneth Copeland. A common text employed in this cause is

Malachi 3.10 (NIV); ' "Bring the whole tithe into the storehouse, that there may food in my house. Test me in this," says the Lord Almighty, "and see if I will not throw open the floodgates of heaven and pour out so much blessing that you will not have room enough for it." ' Another Scripture often used to invoke the idea of a spiritual law is Matthew 25.14–30, which refers to the parable of the talents. The three servants in question are each given some money in trust by their master, with which to look after his interests. When the master returns, the two servants who had invested their money wisely and so gained some interest upon their capital are commended, while the servant who hid his money for fear is given the sharpest of reprimands. The conclusion that some draw from this parable is that if we invest our money in the work of God then it will doubtless be increased in similar proportions to those in the story. What is entirely overlooked is that none of the servants actually owned any of the money, nor earned it for themselves. What they were given, in fact, for their faithfulness, was the privilege of enlarged stewardship and a share of the happiness of their master.

It must also be acknowledged that the Bible does teach a principle about giving and receiving. Jesus clearly said, 'Give, and it will be given unto you. A good measure, pressed down, shaken together and running over, will be poured into your lap. For with the measure you use, it will be measured to you' (Luke 6.38NIV). The apostle Paul, in encouraging the Corinthian Christians to give to the needs of their more needy brethren wrote, 'Whoever sows sparingly will also reap sparingly, and whoever sows generously will also reap generously' (2 Corinthians 9.6f. NIV). Yet it is all too easily overlooked that Jesus was in fact talking about the measure of forgiveness that God gives to the forgiving heart. Paul, in listing some of the rewards of generous giving, nowhere talks about receiving money in return, but about receiving the grace of God to fulfil our needs, or of reaping a harvest of righteousness.

The glib assumption that the blessings in question are material in nature is in sharp contrast to the hard times of life in the New Testament church and its frequent appeals for the poor saints. Florence Bulle points out that even these appeals were not about deserving projects but about destitute people.[2] How often have we heard of leaders who represent some of the larger, renewed churches encouraging their congregations to richer expectations by telling them that as Christians they are children of the King of Kings. David Prior mentions that some of the exponents of prosperity doctrines preach that, as we now live on the other side of Calvary, we can conquer without the necessary sufferings that Jesus had to undergo.[3] This totally disregards the command to take up our cross and follow Christ. It seems that another cross is offering another gospel from that of our Lord Jesus Christ. How different this all is from the encouragements to see that suffering and adversity are the stepping-stones for grace and for character to be formed.[4] Perhaps this tendency to escape from the real cross, which we see far too much of in some renewal circles, explains to some degree why we do not see the development of godly character and depth in some modern-day christians.

One of the largest churches in the world, that under the leadership of Paul Yongi Cho in Seoul, South Korea, has home groups especially for millionaires. A person cannot join unless he has wealth to associate with the élite. This is a far cry from the apostolic church which brought together slaves and governors, fishermen and princes, to the same communion table. This kind of attitude gives rise to the expectation that successful Christian living is normally affluent, befitting the high standards of the well off. Yet our King confessed that he had nowhere to lay his head, and that even foxes and birds of the air had a more secure nest than he.

It seems that prosperity teaching only has appeal in affluent countries. After all, it would hardly have currency on the streets of Calcutta, where Mother Teresa and her army of sisters bring dignity to the dying whose only possessions are the clothes they wear. It has not been preached in the famine-stricken lands of Africa, nor in the war-torn jungles of east Asia. Prosperity doctrines seem to grow up alongside the industrialised and wealthier nations of the developed world, where money talks. This is no surprise to Richard Foster, who believes that behind the concern and interest in money are the invisible spiritual powers that are both seductive and deceptive and which demand an all-embracing devotion to money.[5] 'People jockey to find out what other people earn because in our society, money is a symbol of strength, influence and power.'[6]

Douglas Frank links very closely the growth of the 'Christian' developed nations of Europe and the fact that one of the driving forces behind this success is the so-called Protestant work ethic. This ethic, suggests Frank, gained a new impetus in the late nineteenth century in America which was doing its best to compete with the world and so to come of age. 'It encouraged its adherents to jump into the maelstrom – with both feet and to God's glory – and to view any success achieved as signs of God's favour.'[7] The difficulty with this viewpoint is the casualties who do not make a success of their enterprise. Rather like those who suffered loss in the Old Testament, they were regarded as having been abandoned by God, presumably because of lack of faith, or of some unconfessed sin in their lives. The other kind of casualty, according to Frank, was that the middle-class climber was encouraged to keep his emotions on a tight leash and to cultivate that indomitable will which overcomes all the odds. The result was inhibition and repression, guilt and the stifling of feelings, with the inevitable neurotic consequences. How true this is for the competitive society of Christians who seek to display their rightness with God by the many things they possess or achieve.

So we can see that, while prosperity teachings remind us that serving God does bring its many rewards, these blessings cannot be guaranteed to be material in nature. However, the greatest danger of these teachings is that they distort the relationship between servant and master. Tozer described this as a user society using God: 'Use God to give us safety. Use God to give us peace of mind. Use God to obtain success in business.'[8] Jesus reminded his disciples, just after an argument about who was the most important among them, of the true importance of Christian living. He told them that he had come to serve; they should do likewise. Prosperity teaching appeals to our greed, to the desire to have; while Jesus calls us to give what we have to others, and to follow him.

Prayer Powers

Prayer is the soul's sincere desire,
Uttered or unexpressed,
The motion of a hidden fire
That trembles in the breast.

Prayer is the simplest form of speech
That infant lips can try;
Prayer the sublimest strains that reach
The Majesty on high.

Prayer is the Christian's vital breath,
The Christian's native air,

His watchword at the gates of death;
He enters heaven with prayer.

No prayer is made on earth alone;
The Holy Spirit pleads;
And Jesus on the eternal throne,
For sinners intercedes.

O Thou, by whom we come to God,
The life, the truth, the way,
The path of prayer thyself hast trod:
Lord, teach us how to pray!

James Montgomery

No one will dispute the importance or the necessity of prayer. The whole of Jesus' life and ministry can be seen as prayer. He gives himself to the Father as intercession for the needs of the world; he gives himself to us so that we may be brought to know the Father; and he is the mediator of a new life brought home to our hearts by the Holy Spirit whom he makes available for us. Indeed, the whole fact and possibility of redemption is a consequence of the dialogue and self-giving prayerfulness of the Holy Trinity. The Spirit is sent from the Father through the Son; Jesus draws aside to commune with the Father and openly confesses him before engaging in works of power and miracle. As Jesus praises his Father it is as he rejoices in the Spirit who is with him (Luke 10.21). It is not overstating the case to say that for ourselves, as well as for Jesus, the experience of prayer brings us into an encounter with the Father as well as the Holy Spirit.

Elsewhere in the New Testament we are exhorted and encouraged to pray at all times and in all kinds of ways.[9] There is the command to pray in the Spirit (Ephesians 6.18); and whether this refers explicitly to tongues or not, it does incorporate 'all kinds of prayers and requests'. The letter of James reminds us that the fervent prayers of the righteous are powerful in their effect (5.16).

So far we have been examining prayer as 'task'; something we have been summoned to engage upon in order to see God at work among us. As we shall see shortly, the bringing of prayer into the power game of life largely stems from a misapplication of this concept of prayer. However, there is also prayer as 'gift'. It is interesting to note that the apostle Paul when writing to the various churches invariably begins his letters by stating that he is always praying for them.[10] A closer inspection of some of these texts reveals that the goal of his prayers is that the saints will increase in their knowledge of God. In other words, he is saying that prayer is God's gift and calling into a relationship with himself. So we can see that according to Scripture, prayer is both powerful and purposeful. Unfortunately, there has been an overemphasis upon prayer as task, and resulting from this has been the idea that particular prayer styles or techniques are guaranteed to deliver great results.

An obvious example of this is the recent development of persisting in praise, whatever the circumstances, in order to receive the blessings of God, be they healing or well-being. Now there is no doubt that the Bible places a high priority on praise and worship in the life of the believer. Consider how many of the Psalms guide us to 'praise the Lord'! Perhaps the one which comes most readily to mind is Psalm 150, where every verse is an encouragement to praise God for all the blessings of this life. In the New Testament Paul commands that we are to 'give thanks in all circumstances; for this is the will of God in Christ Jesus for you' (1 Thess. 5.18RSV). Yet this principle of prayer has been taken a stage further by such Christian leaders as Merlin C. Carothers. In his best selling book, *From Prison to Praise*, he points out that the Bible also mentions giving thanks to God 'for' all things as well as 'in' all things (Eph. 5.20). This is basically offering a formula, the adherence to which, no matter what the cost, will bring forth the desired goal. Immediately there is the appeal that here is something I can do which will redeem all my losses and make sense of all my sufferings.

In a later book Carothers gives a number of challenging examples of people who suffered great tragedies but who praised God for what had happened, believing that God's will was in the event and that he was in control of it all. One of these examples concerns a Christian woman who married an alcoholic. For many years she struggled to raise their two children and suffered great anxiety and hardship. The husband indulged in a lifetime of petty crime and was eventually imprisoned. The now destitute wife finally decided to divorce her husband and to try to raise her children in a more stable environment. Upon reading a copy of *From Prison to Praise* she decided to try to improve her life by giving thanks to God for her husband's unfaithfulness and alcoholism: 'Thank you for Al and his drinking,' she prayed. 'Thank you for the years of poverty and fear and loneliness.'[11] The account goes on to tell how the husband was later converted and the couple went on to remarry and lead a new life through faith in Christ. While not wishing to belittle the conversion and happiness of anyone, the clear implication of this kind of testimony is that by the process of praise, God will make all things succeed for us. I hasten to add that this is not necessarily the same thing as God making all things work together for the good of those who are called according to His purposes (Rom. 8.28). The good may well be those hard-earned lessons of humility and holiness that come from times of brokenness and suffering.

The danger of praising for blessing is that we make praise a tool in itself, a technique by which God causes us to succeed against the odds. Consequently many who have tried the route of praise have almost ship-wrecked their faith. Florence Bulle tells of a friend who applied this approach to her growing awareness of homosexuality. Far from finding freedom or healing, this friend began to think of her whole identity in such terms. She was in danger of failing to come into the full picture of what God had for her life.[12]

We must also be careful that when we learn from our losses we do not assume that this is why our losses have come upon us. A well-known Christian writer gives an account of a woman whose ten-year-old daughter had died. She was told that this daughter's death was actually a compliment from God to her. The writer remarked how the woman's expression began to change from grief, to surprise, to a hint of a smile. Then apparently God's compliment, his trust in her, began to fill the void of her loss.[13] The difficulty with this story is that it implies that God is responsible for causing the death of the daughter and that this was a compliment to the woman. Surely this comes very close to making God out to be a cruel tyrant who asks us to praise him for the hurt he causes us. I do not think the writer intended this assumption, but it underlines how very cautious we must be in bringing too easy a solution to the subject of loss or failure.

The assumption that giving thanks for all things brings the blessings we want, needs to be seriously challenged. Far from giving thanks for the sins of the city, Jesus wept over Jerusalem, and prophesied that the consequences of her sinfulness would bring the inevitable judgement. With a similar emotion Paul wrote to the Corinthian church concerning its toleration of sexual sins, 'out of great distress and anguish of heart and with many tears' (2 Cor. 2.4NIV). In fact the whole concept of praise for blessing completely denies the entering into sorrow for sin and suffering which is implicit in Jesus' exhortation for us to be cross-bearers like him. The practice of praise and worship is for giving thanks for who God is and for what he has given us. Whether or not there was going to be any blessed outcome to his praising, Job is on record as saying, 'Though he slay me, yet will I trust him' (Job 13.15).

Tom Smail touches the deeper casualty of such a distortion of prayer when he warns that treating prayer mostly as task means that the central place of the Spirit in the life of worship will almost inevitably be neglected.[14] The Holy Spirit in action is seen as the answer to prayer rather than as the gracious promoter and participator in our prayer. In order to achieve such a good result we adopt ever more fervently new techniques of prayer in the hope that we will reach God's heart. Such a legalistic understanding of the subject puts the focus squarely upon our own efforts, and raises such questions as whether we have enough faith, or live in enough grace, for our prayers to 'get through' and release the power of God. Hence the power of prayer becomes in effect the power of our own faith: communion with God becomes identified with achievement rather than relationship. Indeed, such an approach with prayer starts with the person who prays, and usually ends with the person questioning whether he or she has done enough. We need to recover the aspect of prayer as 'gift' and realise that it is the Holy Spirit himself who brings us to prayer (Eph. 6.18), who addresses the 'Abba' in prayer (Rom. 8.16), and who prays the prayers we cannot (Rom. 8.26–27).

Power Healing

In 1973 I was part of a team which conducted a healing

and evangelistic crusade on the Noctorum council estate on the outskirts of Birkenhead. The evangelist who had been invited to conduct the ministry was Melvin Banks. I found it difficult to identify with the healing aspect of the crusade, which was however carried out in a very balanced way. Therefore I kept myself aloof at the times when people came forward for prayer with the laying on of hands. I was also aware that I did not want to quench the Holy Spirit and get in the way of anyone receiving a healing. However, on one of the quieter afternoons, when I settled down to watch the proceedings, Melvin called me over to work alongside him. I managed to hide my uneasiness as I went ahead of him asking people about the needs for which they wanted healing. Eventually we came to a young girl about eight years old who was accompanied by her mother. This girl had apparently been born deaf. Immediately the need was shared with Melvin, he placed the index fingers of his hands into each ear of the girl. I felt taken aback and just wanted to be somewhere else. Somehow this proximity to praying for healing made me feel weak and exposed and doubting, and I wanted to escape. The prayer was quite short, and Melvin then went and stood behind the girl and began to speak her name. Her response was immediate and overwhelmed me. She began to turn around in acknowledgement of the sound, and I shall never forget the look on her face, which was a mixture of pain and growing awareness that she could hear. Her mother burst into tears and openly wept aloud with astonishment. I cannot remember much else about the occasion except for the fact that I had to get away on my own and confess to God my weakness and need of him.

Such an experience, and others beside, leave me in no doubt that God can and does heal people today. Furthermore it is also true that the church has been called and commissioned to be a healing community. Of course, this must not be divorced from the proclamation of the kingdom of God. Hence the ministry of healing is to be part of the sharing of the good news of the love of God (cf. Matt. 10.5–8; Luke 10.1, 9; and Mark 16.18–20). The difficulties and distortions occur when we forget this and begin to focus upon healing as a separate and individual item. The context of proclamation enables us to understand healing as an element in our journey to wholeness and to realise and accept that although we may not see all the healings we want, it is journey's end which is the greater goal. The issue was brought home to me rather emphatically with the differing opinions concerning the death of David Watson.

In his book *Fear No Evil*, David wrote that he believed that God would heal him. Alas, this was not o be, despite the fact that Christians around the world were praying for his recovery. Many, though sad at the death of such a gifted preacher and teacher, accepted this, trusting that God had a fuller purpose in mind for David. Others however, such as John Wimber and some associate ministers of the Vineyard Fellowship, are alleged to have said that in this particular battle against sickness, the Devil won and David Watson lost because his faith was not big enough. The assumption behind this latter idea is that failure in healing is a failure in faith. What is more disturbing is the association of the triumph of evil with the persistence of a sickness.

Because healing has been separated from proclamation, the sight and significance of heaven has been lost from view. Surely for the Christian, death is the greatest healing of all until we see the coming of Christ in the clouds! Far from David Watson's death being a failure of faith, it seems that this attitude towards healing is a failure to understand the triumph of Christian death and the conquest of the grave. Even Lazarus, who I am sure astounded the congregation in his local synagogue when he worshipped there for the first time after his raising from the dead, grew old and eventually died.

Therefore it seems that we must recognise that one of the problems of believing and expecting God to heal is the danger of intolerance with those whose wounds do not seem to heal. We may think that they have not enough faith, or are continuing in some sin. The effect of this reasoning is to shift the responsibility for lack of healing on to the sufferer. Yet should we be carrying the responsibility for healing in the first place? If we have been commanded by the Lord Jesus to preach the good news and to accompany that with the ministry of prayer for healing, then the question is one of obedience or disobedience to a divine command to serve the needs of others. The consequences of our obedience and faith, whether they result in healing or no improvement at all, belong to God and not to us.

However, because God is ultimately responsible for healing, this means that we need not approach this ministry with hidden agenda such as wanting to look good or successful. We can in fact be liberated into an openness and honesty about our failures. Consider the circumstances of the prophet Elisha who was confronted by the anger of the Shunammite woman whose son had died. She virtually accused him of being responsible for the lad's death and blamed the prophet for raising her hopes of motherhood in the first place. It is as if the original healing, that of enabling an infertile woman to conceive and have a child, had all come to a sad end. Elisha, far from trying to maintain his equilibrium in public, simply confesses that he is ignorant of the facts and does not know what to do. He says to his servant who is anxious to remove the woman and possibly save some of his own embarrassment, 'Leave her alone!

Can't you see, she is in bitter distress and the Lord has hidden it from me and has not told me why.' (2 Kings 4.27 TEV) It is also instructive to notice that despite this lack of knowledge and two further instances of no apparent healing in response to his prayers, the prophet was still free to persist in prayer and did finally see the miracle of healing for the boy.

Another benefit from seeing that healing is the ultimate prerogative of God is that we can come to prayer in weakness. This is in contrast to books with such titles as *Power Healing* which seem to appeal much more to the spirit of the successful man of this age than to the spirit of Calvary. Certainly God has power to heal, but I think that we are sometimes seduced into preoccupation with such power rather than with that power (of love) which is made perfect through our weakness.

If we are honestly to engage in the ministry of healing then we need to take to heart those words of Dietrich Bonhoeffer: 'When Christ calls a man, he bids him come and die.'[15] The more we pray for healing the more we shall see healing but we shall also encounter the heartache of unanswered prayers. Here lies the mystery of God's power through us; the Holy Spirit brings us deeper into vulnerability and conflict. The temptation is to try and keep everything in a neat equation where everything on one side balances out with the other. Christian ministry is not so easily managed. Let us then be open and believing in our God and Father to help and heal those whom we bring to him, yet let us not evade the failures and mysteries that will also come. Whatever our present miracles and successes, failures and questions, they are all pointers to the greater reality of being made complete in the presence of Christ when he returns or calls us to his side.

Conclusion

> We must not show ourselves to be striving after spiritual consolations; come what may, the great thing for us to do is to embrace the cross. *Teresa of Avila*

So we can see that these distortions of truth do not really constitute some new form of heresy but rather reflect an anxiety concerning failures in Christian experience. It is indicative of our need to encounter God and his power and to safely account for any loss or failure which are shown to be only a part of God's winning ways for our lives. Of course there is absolutely nothing wrong with a desire to experience the power of God, indeed Jesus himself promised us power (*dunamis*) when the Holy Spirit comes upon us (Acts 1.8). However, it is when we make our experience of power the basis for meaning and security in our faith that we are liable to lose our spiritual balance. It can become like a drug which distorts our sense of reality and so we become obsessive about encountering power and unable to handle failure. For Donald Bloesch, this form of 'enthusiasm' is like seeking after a premature redemption. 'They see themselves not as pilgrims journeying to a foreign land, but as initiates into the higher mysteries of the faith.'[16] This may be overstating the issue for many of us, but it rightly pinpoints our preoccupation with the 'now' at the expense of the 'not yet'.

We are living in days when the Holy Spirit is bringing renewal to the life of the church. There is a recovery of the spiritual gifts and powers which, when used in conjunction with the preaching of the gospel, are bringing new life and healing to many. There is an expectancy in the air that God is doing great things and that there is much more to come. There is a great deal of talk of imminent revival. Conferences are held in which people are taught how to expect signs and wonders as a regular

49

feature of their evangelism. There are in fact twelve references in the Acts of the Apostles to signs and wonders accompanying the witness of the church (see p. 61). The church is also recovering its God-given authority to cast out demonic spirits in the name of Jesus Christ. Recently prophecy has become a subject which is challenging many to be open to the voice of God speaking directly to them. Praise the Lord for what he is doing – and how we long to see more and more people converted to Christ and brought into fullness of life and power by the Holy Spirit.

However, this is not the whole story. There is unbelief and rejection of the good news and hostility towards the church. In a news item in *Renewal* magazine (November 1990), Dr David Barrett showed that over the last ten years the number of Christian martyrs has been 260,000. By the year 2000 the number could well rise to half a million. In all our openness to God in power we must also be open to the crucified God who calls us to take up our cross and follow him. Therefore we dare not try to juggle with our failures by 'spiritualising' them into some form of secret success because this is to deny the cross itself. As we shall see in the next chapter, people of faith, including Jesus himself, had to learn how to handle failure whilst still keeping the faith.

No Scar?

Hast thou no scar?
No hidden scar on foot, or side or hand?
I hear thee sung as mighty in the land,
I hear them hail thy bright ascendent star,
Hast thou no scar?

Hast thou no wound?
Yet I was wounded by the archers, spent,
Leaned me against a tree to die; and rent
By ravening beasts that compassed me,
    I swooned:
Hast thou no wound?

No wound? No scar?
Yet, as the master shall the servant be,
And pierced are the feet that follow me;
But thine are whole: can he have travelled far
Who has no wound nor scar?

Amy Wilson Carmichael[17]

4 SIGNS AND WONDERS AND FAILURES

'If you want to be successful you don't study people who have been a failure.' *Bob Schwartz*[1]

Bob Schwartz's words beg the question of why we read the Bible. The answer may say more about the reader's own agenda than present a balanced summary of the Scriptures. Some may see in its pages one long story of triumph and conquest, from the destruction by Israel of nations far outnumbering them to the defeat of demonic powers by Jesus as he died for our sins upon the cross. Others see the journey of life represented as a vale of tears where we can expect no more than to take up our cross and follow the suffering servant, Jesus Christ: it is only escaped by faith's triumph over death, or the return of Jesus Christ at his second coming.

However, the basic consensus of the Scriptures themselves indicates that they are written not that we may merely triumph or faithfully suffer but that we may believe on Jesus Christ and enter into his quality of life for us (cf. John 20.30–31). When the apostle Paul wrote to Timothy to give him advice about how to lead his church forward, he spoke of God's word being given so that they might live a holy and good life: 'You have known the holy Scriptures, which are able to make you wise for salvation through faith in Christ Jesus. All Scripture is God-breathed and is useful for teaching, rebuking, correcting and training in righteousness, so that the man of God may be thoroughly equipped for every good work' (2 Tim. 3.16f. NIV).

Rather than giving a mandate for power, Paul implies

that the Word is primarily a mandate for holiness. At heart the Scriptures teach us to desire goodness rather than greatness. In the parable of the sower Jesus teaches that the seed is the word, the offer of sharing in a quality of life that only God can give (Mark 4.1–20). This word is the call to a life which challenges the fallen standards and priorities of the secular age and is not therefore well received by the majority. It is not a call to power, but to godliness.

However, there are times when the word is seen to be very powerful. Jeremiah describes the word of God as like a hammer which breaks rocks into pieces (Jer. 23.29). The writer to the Hebrews (presuming this to be Paul) tells how the word has the power to separate the unseparable, dividing soul and spirit, joints and marrow (Heb. 4.12–13). Both of these testimonies to power speak of the word as confronting and exposing the darkness and evil within the world. Yet there is a price to pay for this kind of power. Both Jeremiah and Paul suffered for wielding powerful words in public. Jeremiah ended his days in obscurity amongst a scattered band of escaping terrorists in Egypt and Paul was beheaded in Rome.

Jesus embodies all the principles of the written word because he is the living Word, and as such is described as being full of grace and truth (John 1.14). He models in his life the same pattern of the word in the Old Testament. His call to repentance and to receiving the good news is a call to holiness. He challenges and exposes the evil and darkness within the world. He demonstrates this ability to confront it, not only by his amazing wisdom and authority in debate and dialogue but by healing every kind of disease and casting out demons. And like the word of the Old Testament he also pays the price of his confrontation. But though he suffers, because he is the unique son of God, he converts his suffering into an offer and resource for salvation. Yet we must not glibly assume that because he is able to do this, his suffering is cosmetic, that somehow his divinity shields him from the full impact of pain and failure. Such a Christ is of no use to Christians who struggle with failure and its often unanswered problems. As Paul clearly states, we do have a high priest in Jesus who is able to touch the feelings of our experiences because he was tested just like us (Heb. 4.15).

In a later chapter we shall examine more closely Jesus' own experience of failure and compare how that speaks to ours. For now we conclude that the word itself calls us firstly to holiness, and that its call to power has the strong price of suffering. When I was a student a missionary conference was held every year in a huge tent which was erected in the college grounds. One of the banners hung around the walls read, 'For the old time power there is the old time price.' I used to be amused by this banner, because it represented for me the old worn-out traditions of the college. Now I regret my arrogance, for I have learned that God's word proclaims itself to be a word of power and pain for those who will live by it.

Bob Schwartz, quoted at the beginning of this chapter, would probably not include the Bible on his reading list. Right after the account of the wonders of God's creation there comes the fatal flaw of human disobedience and the horror of rebellion in paradise. Neither is the history of God's chosen people a proud one; a great hero like Noah is found drunk and disorderly, and a man after God's own heart like King David commits murder in order to try and cover up his adultery. Moses could lead a vagabond people and forge them into something approaching a cohesive nation. His faith took him into the waters of the Red Sea to find safe passage across while the Egyptian army perished. He handled the daily burdens of administration on a scale that would defy the competence of a council office workforce. Yet he suddenly ran out of patience in relying upon God and failed as a consequence to enter the land of promise. Think of the power in the prophetic ministries of Elijah and John the Baptist. Yet Elijah ran from the threats of a queen and wished to die alone. John the Baptist ended up in prison and unsure of who Jesus was, even after twice proclaiming him in public as the Lamb of God who takes away the sins of the world.

These are not the whitewashed characters of religious propaganda, but gifted people who none the less fail and fall into sin. Schwartz's doctrine would lead us to conclude that worth is only for those who succeed; or worse still, to brush aside our failures and what they have to teach us about our basic nature and choices in life as we pursue the elusive grail of success. We imagine that we are more perfect than we are and take an idealised view of human nature. The tragedy is that many use religion for this end. It has been said that 'Often we use religion to anaesthetise ourselves from the living God, living in a make-believe world of ecclesiastical goings on that protect us from the risk of naked faith and the vulnerability of love, which is what the real world of Christian living is all about.'[2]

So from the beginning the Bible points out how God's creation is wounded and undermined by the fallen nature of his most prized creation, men and women. We are capable of many great and beautiful things but we also have the potential to destroy and devour the very world. Yet running like a thread through the scriptural record, is the need for people to recognise their need of and dependence upon God. This is, after all, what lies at the heart of Christ's call to repentance; this is what made him so challenging and confrontational, and so dangerous to the religious authorities. A typical example of this is the healing of the man lowered through the roof of the house where Jesus was teaching. There was the expectation of physical healing but first Jesus offered a healing which no other could give, that of forgiveness. Perhaps upon hearing these words the paralytic knew that this was the root of all his problems and the primary healing that he needed. For the teachers of the law who were present, perhaps it challenged their need for healing of heart because they prided themselves on their ability to know the ways of God and it exposed their arrogance and need as being equal to that of the paralytic. Jesus's words of forgiveness force all of us to look within at the frailty and corruption of our souls. In the words of Douglas Frank:

> The call to repentance is not a call to be sorry for a few glaring imperfections in an otherwise perfect creation. Nor is it a call to repent once and be made whole in some straightforward way that will make further repentance unnecessary. Who would not opt for that kind of repentance? It offers the very godlikeness for which we all hunger. The biblical notion of repentance has to do rather with a recognition that in our very essence we are not now – nor ever shall be – anything but sinners with whom Jesus chose to eat. Biblical repentance attacks that secret fortress inside where we have established a place to nest in this world, where we have created an illusion of safety. It topples the house of cards that protects our self-esteem. It rips from our eyes the blinders that hide our own frail mortality from our own view.[3]

So at one basic but fundamental level we learn that by studying the failures of both the godly and the ungodly within the Bible we see our need for true repentance and dependence upon God. This is the beginning of our healing and our journey into wholeness of life. After all, it was Jesus who said that his healing and salvation were only possible for those who recognised their own sickness of heart and their need of the healing Christ (Mark 2.17). As we continue to study the Scriptures we see that there are certain themes which begin to emerge which imply a call and commission to fail.

The Call to Limited Effectiveness

Maria Boulding, in her book *Gateway to Hope*, speaks of the call to prophetic failure for the eighth-century prophets.[4] She refers in particular to Isaiah's call to ministry, which incidentally was accompanied by a great vision of the cleansing power of God. Yet at the core of this prophetic call was the reminder that the response to his work would be one of the hardening of hearts and a growing disinterest among the people.

> Then I heard the voice of the Lord saying, 'Whom shall I send? And who will go for us?' And I said, 'Here am I send me!' He said, 'Go and tell this people: "Be ever hearing, but never understanding; be ever seeing, but never perceiving." Make the heart of this people calloused; make their ears dull and close their eyes. Otherwise they might see with their eyes, hear with their ears, understand with their hearts, and turn and be healed' (Isa. 6.8–10NIV).

Hardly an encouraging start for this court visionary! And yet he accepts the commission.

Jeremiah did not fare much better. He suffered imprisonment for his faithfulness and saw a whole collection of his prophecies cut up and burned (Jer. 36.23). He is often called 'the moaning prophet', perhaps unfairly. He freely expresses his hurt feelings to God and yet goes on with his work and from time to time flashes of vision come to him of a day when, despite the odds, God will have a faithful remnant at last in the land of Israel;

> O Lord, you deceived me and I was deceived; you overpowered me and prevailed. I am ridiculed all day long, everyone mocks me . . . So the word of the Lord has brought me insult and reproach all day long . . . But the Lord is with me like a mighty warrior . . . Sing to the Lord! Give praise to the Lord! He rescues the life of the needy from the hand of the wicked. (Jer. 20.7–13NIV)

Space prevents us from studying the rather bizarre call to Hosea to marry a woman who would obviously be unfaithful to him. And yet his failed marriage and his perseverance in loving his recalcitrant wife becomes an illustration of God's commitment to continue loving those who fail to be faithful. Of all the prophets it seems that only a handful, such as Elijah and Elisha, could be said to be powerful and successful. Perhaps the most effective of them was in fact the most reluctant – Jonah, who ran from God's call precisely because he knew God's capabilities to save the hated citizens of Nineveh. When Jesus summarised Israel's reaction to the prophets he talked in terms of the people stoning them! With the benefit of hindsight we can see how their words were like seeds planted in the ground which now provide us with a rich treasury of guidance; but they themselves were not so fortunate. Similarly, we may not see any point to our own failure, but this is when we are especially to tell God how it feels and then trust our lives and limitations into hands more capable than our own.

The same theme of limited effectivity runs through the ministry of the New Testament church. There is the startling admission that the unbelief of some people prevented Jesus from exercising his power to do miracles (Matt. 13.58) This may help us to account for some of our failures; but it also raises the bigger question of why God should allow our effectiveness to depend on other peoples' responses. No answer is given. Paul, writing to the Corinthians, contrasts his own experiences of power and limitation:

> We have this treasure (i.e. the knowledge of God's glory) in jars of clay to show that this all-surpassing power is from God and not from us. We are hard pressed on every side, but not crushed; perplexed but not in despair; persecuted but not abandoned; struck down but not destroyed. (2 Cor. 4.7–10NIV)

In one breath Paul talks about the excellency of God's power in his ministry and in the next he catalogues the failures and hardships despite his possession of this power. Ultimately this experience of power was to lead Paul into prison and death. Peter escaped miraculously from prison but the saintly James was beheaded with the sword, his days of promise rudely cut down (Acts 12). All that personal teaching and time given to James by Jesus, and he never seemed to have the chance to show his undoubted abilities! The same might be said of countless eager missionaries who confidently went to distant countries to serve God, only to perish from diseases in the first few months.

Is it unreasonable to expect God to intervene and protect us from failure or disaster? Yet failure is written into the heart of the Gospel, for the one who is the good news himself faced limitations and failure. And there are hundreds of Christians who, though not knowing why things went wrong, learned that God had promised to be with them in their dark times and that the knowledge of this was more prized than knowing why they failed.

In December 1990 my wife and I were in Ethiopia in the home of the ex-mayor of Addis Ababa and his wife Gemba. They had both been imprisoned in 1976, following the military coup that ousted Haile Selassie from power. They spent over six years apart and their young children had to be smuggled out of the country. The ex-mayor daily stood in the prison compound and listened to the names called out of those who were to be executed, fully expecting his name to be on the list – an expectation which ended only on the day of his release eight years later. Meanwhile their property had been confiscated and friends had to come and feed them in their separate prisons if they were not to starve. I asked them what the experience had given them. Sister Gemba, as she is known, confessed that she was bitter at first at losing all the privileges they had had, but in time came to be thankful for the opportunity to learn and practise the presence of God. The experience has given her a joy in serving God and the people of her nation, despite their political persuasions. She told me that she had given up trying to work out why God had taught them through the vehicle of suffering and failure. Gemba had realised that the call of God to follow Christ includes also the call to limited expectations. Some of these failures and limitations will never be explained but we must press through this and make sure that we hold on to the reality of God's abiding presence with us.

David Watson told of an encounter which underlines this whole issue of limited expectations.

When I was recently in Montreal I met a wonderful black Christian from Uganda called Henry. Henry was one day travelling with his friend on a 'bus in Uganda when they were ambushed by guerillas. Shots were fired and Henry had half his face blown away from the nose downwards. It was a miracle that he survived at all. A Christian organisation called World Vision paid for him to go to Montreal, a city famous for its outstanding medical school, and covered the fees necessary to rebuild Henry's face. When I first saw him he had many more operations to come, and I could not help flinching when I saw the mask that had once been a face. His eyes, however, still sparkled. Since Henry was quite unable to speak he wrote these words, 'God never promises us an easy time. Just safe arrival.'[5]

A final word needs to be said on the subject of our limited expectations. John Wimber has pioneered an approach to ministry based on signs and wonders. It is a charismatic approach, with the expectation that God will give a word of knowledge or a vision or some spiritual perception of particular needs amongst the fellowship. These words are shared publicly or privately with the intention of offering prayer ministry for healing. Very often the impact of such a ministry is very powerful and there are numerous reports and testimonies of healing, renewal of faith, and an increased expectancy for God to act in power.[6]

The term 'signs and wonders' is not a newly-coined phrase to describe a new technique of ministry but, as mentioned earlier, is to be found on at least twelve occasions in the Acts of the Apostles. We may group them as follows in so far as they refer to an individual's ministry: Jesus (2.22; 4.30); Paul and Barnabas (15.12; 19.11ff.; 14.3); Stephen (6.8); Peter and John (4.16); Philip (8.6; 8.13); Apostles (2.43; 5.12); Moses (7.36).

All of the individuals listed here, with the exception of Philip, suffered in some way and their ministry, despite the power, was rejected and their lives were forfeited.

Paul and Barnabas worked side by side as they saw great signs and wonders, and yet they argued and Barnabas returned home, his work as a pioneer missionary at an end. Stephen had barely begun his years of promise when he was brutally stoned to death.

However, we must not be tempted to conclude that we must choose between signs and wonders or failure. Neither can we make a case, as some try to do for the charismatic gifts, that these powers were only for the apostolic age. The truth of the matter is that we are called to experience both aspects, and this is the balance found in those who would take up their cross and follow Jesus. Our modern church has confused the call to power with the secular gospel of success. The early Christians were enabled to work great miracles, but the cost was high, and what is more they were willing to pay it. It is said that all power corrupts, and this can be true even of spiritual power. It is true that such signs and wonders facilitated the preaching of the gospel as our examples indicate but there is always the danger of a Simon Magus wanting the power for his own prestige.

The Call to Wounded Leadership

It was Frank Lake in his book *Clinical Theology* who remarked that the great thing about the disciples was not that they were men of such great faith but that they were such honest doubters. They stumble around in the Gospels with more than a hint of the resurrection before them, and still fail to see or understand the implications of what Jesus told them on numerous occasions. Those who considered themselves to be close friends of his failed to recognise him after the resurrection, even though he was still the same and carried the marks of his crucifixion for everyone to see. Perhaps the most striking example of this is the account of the two on the

Emmaus Road who had Jesus as a walking companion for a few miles (Luke 24.13–35). I am sure that Luke recounts this story with a touch of humour. When the stranger asks them what they are discussing they begin by telling him how powerful Jesus' ministry was, and of his arrest and crucifixion by the chief priests and the Roman authorities. Then they go on to say that it is now the third day since all this happened, that some women had reported that the body was absent from the tomb and that angels were there proclaiming that Jesus was alive; and that others have corroborated the womens' story. Yet with all of this information they are still walking away from the scene of God's mighty actions with their hearts full of sadness and doubt. Hardly a flattering recommendation for those who had been called to be his witnesses!

Yet it is precisely those who know themselves to be weak who are called to be channels of God's grace and power. It is for this reason that Brendan Byrne is happy to accept the shorter ending to Mark's Gospel which ends with the verse, 'Trembling and bewildered, the women went out and fled from the tomb. They said nothing to anyone because they were afraid' (Mark 16.8). Byrne writes, 'We are immeasurably in Mark's debt that he confronted so unflinchingly the fact of failure, that by keeping at bay any sense of a "happy ending", he let the failure and the fear stand in stark relief.'[7]

However, the first disciples were soon being swept into a kingdom of their own making. James and John, at their mother's instigation, had asked Jesus for a place on either side of him when he was to come in his conquering power (Mark 10.35–45). When Jesus, looking forward to Calvary, asked them if they could drink the cup he was about to be given they glibly answered that they could. After this unpromising beginning they were nevertheless given teaching and training by Jesus and there was a marked transformation in them. James became a martyr, surrendering his life not for a throne but for the gospel; and John lived on into old age, writing letters full of love for Christ. This is a recurring theme for discipleship. No matter what our hopes and expectations, Jesus calls us to his cross, and true discipleship begins from there. To return to Douglas Frank's analogy of the nest (p. 56), as disciples we encounter a Christ who disturbs and dismantles our expectations of achievement. He tumbles us from our home-made nests and wounds our pride and false expectations.

Perhaps the call and training of Peter is the best example of this process. Here is a strong character who seems larger than life and not afraid to speak his mind. He is full of ideas and visions of what could be. His feelings are always near the surface and he freely pours them out. When he reluctantly and rather arrogantly accepts Jesus' advice about fishing on the opposite side of his boat and to his amazement pulls in a large catch of fish, he immediately repents and openly confesses his sinfulness (Luke 5.4–11). His innate optimism more often than not proved to be an obstacle to his spiritual growth. He was called to be the undisputed leader of the emerging church but his training involved a transformation through wounding. There are three moments when this call to wounded leadership is particularly apparent. On the mountain of transfiguration, when something of the eternal glory of God shines through Jesus Christ and the dead saints Elijah and Moses come to talk, it is Peter who suggests a way of making this mountain-top glory permanent. His dream of permanence is shattered by the cloud which sweeps aside his fantasies and focuses his attention on Jesus, and when he comes down from the mountain only to find the rest of the disciples wrestling with their failure to deliver someone from evil (Mark 9.2–9, 14f.).

The second moment follows close upon Peter receiving a revelation from God as to the real identity of Jesus as the Christ of God. Seconds later Jesus begins to reveal the ordeal and sacrifices which lie before him. Peter intervenes and declares that he will protect Jesus from his ignominious failure. Perhaps his ego is inflated with his recent experience of being given such a word of knowledge from the Father. But Peter is sharply rebuked and his desire to protect Jesus is exposed as a sort of smothering love which is more typical of the Devil than a saint (Matt. 16.15–23).

The third moment is the moment of professed allegiance coupled with the time of strong denial. In the upper room and during their last meal together, Jesus speaks again of his forthcoming death and obliquely refers to his betrayer Judas. It is Peter, raising his voice above all the rest, who firmly declares that he will defend Jesus from all comers. He seems to have forgotten his previous moment of smothering the Christ. It is more than likely that Peter meant what he said, but none the less Jesus tells him that he will in fact deny him. Events proved Christ's word to be prophetic. Peter, true to his word, takes out his sword when the gang arrives to arrest Jesus but is halted in his actions. He is able to handle the big, public moments, but it is when he is alone that he cannot cope. So when he is on his own by the fire being quizzed by a curious servant girl, he weakly blasphemes and denies any knowledge of Jesus. Later, as he meets Jesus after his resurrection and they share a meal by the seaside, Peter is asked again and again if he loves him. Interestingly enough the word used on this occasion for the fire they stood by is *anthrakia*, the same word used by John for the charcoal fire by which Peter had denied his Lord (John 18.18; 21.15–19). We can only imagine the thoughts running through Peter's mind as he stood by that familiar fire and affirmed his love for Christ. It was a time for healing his past and releasing him from the power of his rash words. Jesus closed his conversation with Peter with the same words he spoke when he first met him, 'Follow me.' Peter was recommissioned to serve, and it was now that Jesus spoke of the sacrificial price Peter would pay in following him.

This call to wounded leadership is not just peculiar to Peter. It is characteristic of the call to all Christians to take up their cross and follow Christ. The purpose of this is not to deny us the power of the Spirit but that we may be conformed to the image of the Son and learn to be vulnerable and open to the will of God for our lives. Neither is it a destroying of our character, but a channelling of powers into Calvary living. Henri Nouwen aptly sums up this theme:

> The most important quality of Christian leadership is not leadership of power and control, but one of powerlessness and humility in which the suffering servant of God, Jesus Christ, is made manifest . . . a leadership in which power is constantly abandoned in favour of love. Powerlessness and humility in the spiritual life do not refer to people who have no spine . . . They refer to people who are so deeply in love with Jesus that they are ready to follow him where he guides them.[8]

The Call to Suffer

Recently leaders of a group called Life Sharers declared that they were never going to die. They appeared on television to proclaim their doctrines and despite questions about their obvious ageing, maintained that it was a flaw of Christian teaching which had created the obsession with death. They believed that there was no

66

resurrection because there was no death.[9] Members of this sect who were interviewed shared how their lives had increased in quality and joy now that they had realised that they need not die. All hardship had seemingly been swept aside as they had now entered upon the good life. While we may be tempted to dismiss this group as cranks we need to take note of the underlying issue, which is a rejection of God's call to us to suffer in the name of Christ.

This call to suffering is made abundantly plain in the New Testament. It is not presented as an option for those who are more spiritual than others, it is mandatory for Christian living: 'To this you were called, because Christ suffered for you, leaving you an example, that you should follow in his steps' (1 Pet. 2.21NIV). Both of Peter's epistles are written for those who are suffering persecution and who may be wondering what on earth has gone wrong with their faith that everything appears to be failing (cf. 1 Pet. 4.12f.). Paul speaks of Christian suffering as a calling and a privilege: 'It has been granted to you on behalf of Christ not only to believe on him, but also to suffer for him' (Phil. 1.29NIV). He wrote to his protégé Timothy that it is by the power of God that we are able to experience suffering (2 Tim. 1.8). He also coupled suffering with godliness and glory. This is the fellowship into which God has called us in Christ, and there is no other route to glory because it is the way of Christ.[10]

If we would be true disciples then we must take up the cross of suffering and rejection. Just as Jesus can be the effective Christ for us precisely because of his suffering and rejection, so we can only be a redemptive presence in this fallen world if we join him in these sufferings and rejections. Dietrich Bonhoeffer eloquently summed up the necessity of redemptive suffering in Christ and his church:

Suffering has to be endured in order that it may pass away. Either the world must bear the whole burden and collapse beneath it, or it must fall on Christ to be overcome in him. He therefore suffers vicariously for the world. His is the only suffering which has redemptive efficacy. But the Church knows that the world is still seeking for someone to bear its sufferings, and so, as it follows Christ, suffering becomes the Church's lot too and bearing it, it is borne up by Christ. As it follows him beneath the cross, the Church stands before God as the representative of the world.[11]

Suffering may come in many forms: persecution, rejection, misunderstanding, or giving up something loved in order to be free to follow. Whatever it is, we cannot determine its nature because it is God who calls us to suffer. Therefore it is only as we take up our cross of commitment that we can suffer the loss of things and still be free to serve.

Another important lesson to learn is that we do not suffer alone. We are part of the body of Christ, and even when we are well and are seeing the power of God in our lives we must not lose sight of others who suffer. The writer to the Hebrews devotes a whole chapter to men and women of faith. What is remarkable is that he gives, side by side, a list of those who triumphed against all odds through their faith as well as a list of those who had faith to fail. He is anxious to stress that it is the same faith at work in both circumstances. It is not as if those who defeated their enemies succeeded with faith and those who died had not enough faith to overcome their battles. 'These were all commended for their faith, yet none of them received what had been promised. God had planned something better for us so that *only together with us* would they be made perfect' (Heb. 11.39–40).

The writer lifts our horizons above the immediate to the eschatalogical hope itself. He says, in effect, that we need the fellowship of those who have failed if we are going to complete God's picture of a redeemed society. For whether we succeed or fail in our Christian walk, the real issue is that we are being 'made perfect' as we stay focused upon the Christ who is both powerful and also helpless upon the cross.

Sheila Cassidy picks up this idea of the helplessness of the suffering of Christ and asks us to consider, 'What ministry can we offer him there?' I once put this question to a Pentecostal church when I was in the middle of preaching a sermon. At first there was a silence and then one of their elders with great conviction said loudly, 'Nothing.' Cassidy calls this the spirituality of the foot of the cross, the stance of the impotent bystander.[12] There will be many times in our lives when we will face the suffering of an unhealed body or mind, be it ours or another's. There will be occasions when we will be sorely oppressed and our faith ready to collapse. It is just at these times when friends or ministers will be ready with their advice, but very often it does not begin to answer our questions. What is it we can offer at these moments of powerlessness? Nothing, but to watch and pray. This may not end the suffering, but it prevents the sufferer from being isolated and alone. Thanks to the love of his mother and friends, Jesus was not alone when his hour of suffering came. He calls us to suffering so that we may go and do likewise.

> Slowly as the years go by, I learn about the importance of powerlessness. The secret is not to be afraid of it – not to run away. The dying know we are not God . . . All they ask is that we do not desert them: that we stand our ground at the foot of the cross. At this stage of the journey, of being there, of simply being; it is, in many ways, the hardest part.[13]

In concluding this chapter we need to consider briefly suffering and the problem of evil. Often in Scripture the question was asked why evil-doers prospered while the suffering saints saw no end to their problems. The prophet Habakkuk knew what it was to live in the midst of the evil. He was depressed by the violence and destruction he saw, and how the people disregarded God's law. He saw the apparent impotence of the few who tried to live righteous lives in a wicked city. He even doubted if God cared for the righteous, and voiced his fears: 'How long, O Lord, must I cry for help and you do not listen? Or cry out to you, "Violence!" but you do not save?' (Hab. 1.2NIV).

There were two basic responses in popular thought to the problem of evil for the righteous person. One was that even though the evil man seems to prosper, a day of reckoning will come in the next world if not in this. The other was to become more dependent upon seeing signs of God in action in order to demonstrate that no matter how bad things might look, our God reigns. While both of these ideas do contain some truth, the danger lies in the way we become obsessive about explaining why we see suffering. A third response to the issue of suffering for the unrighteous was simply to dismiss it as the effects of a sinful life. In the book of Job we see a story of how these assumptions clashed, in the failure of four counsellors to convince their client about why he was suffering. The more they failed in their ministry to Job, the more their own world of faith began to totter. We shall look at this failing in ministry in the final chapter of this book. First, we consider Jesus' own experience of failure.

5 *CHRIST AND A CROSS FOR FAILURES*

The other gods were strong,
but thou wast weak;
They rode, but thou
didst stagger to a throne.

But to our wounds
only God's wounds can speak,
And not a god has wounds
but Thou alone.

Edward Shillito[1]

Sheila Cassidy in her book *Good Friday People* mentions those people in particular who are very specially loved by God because he has called them to walk towards him along a certain narrow path – the road to Calvary.[2] It is of course the same road taken by the Son of God as he went on his journey of life and death. There is no romance or nostalgia on this Calvary road, for it is the way of loss and suffering. Cassidy goes on to identify two results of this journey. Some of the walkers are purified and strengthened and go on to do great things for God. The others are quite simply broken, stripped bare and destroyed. Christ, it seems – and this is our ultimate healing – embraces both results. So it is that Jesus calls us to take up our cross and to follow him. In doing so, he reminds us that the cross is not some temporary spiritual dark night of the soul which, once endured leads us on into better times of success and maturity; the cross is a continuous experience of living with suffering and failure. Dom Dominic Gaisford

71

wrote that it is in this sense that Christianity is a religion of failure, whereas we want and expect it to be a recipe for living our lives happily and contentedly.[3] What Gaisford is underlining is the need to stay vulnerable and open to life in the raw, rather than using Christianity as some form of escapism into a 'happy ever after' story more familiar in fairy tales than in true gospel living. According to Gaisford it is this demand to stay vulnerable that is implicit in facing the cross. Jesus, in his earthly life, refused to dodge the call of the cross for an easy life of unstoppable power. He suffered all the dissatisfactions of being misunderstood and misjudged by friends, family and enemies alike. 'His was an unrequited love on a massive scale that must have amounted to an almost intolerable experience for him of loneliness and failure.' Yet Jesus is not wishing to deny moments of power; but he does bring them all into the focus of the greater reality of the cross, the Calvary lifestyle.

Luke, in his Gospel, points up the contrast of Jesus going from the mountain-top experience to the ignominy of the cross. Jesus sits on the Mount of Transfiguration with the great saints of the Old Testament period, Moses and Elijah. His disciples sit in awe as they see something of Christ's majesty shine through his face. Before the chapter is completed Jesus has 'resolutely set out for Jerusalem'. (9.51) The passage implies that there were many distractions or high moments that Jesus could have held on to, but no, he had to go to Jerusalem and embrace his cross. Jesus never lost sight of the importance of the cross which lay before him and to this end he would even burst in on the joy of his disciples and endeavour to prepare them for what was to come both for himself and them. (cf. Matt. 16.16ff.)

At apparently the peak of success, Jesus talks about the cross. He is saying that the focus for Christian power as well as for suffering has to be the fact and event of his cross. Everything in the disciples' experience must align itself with this significant moment of Calvary. Every success must be brought to his cross; every issue of suffering, whether it leads to insight or is stuck in pain, must be brought to the cross. We cannot explain completely why God asks this of us, but surely it is primarily because at Calvary God demonstrates most powerfully, and in the greatest weakness, his abiding presence in times of overcoming and times of suffering. Both triumph and torture are brought to balance at this place where God chooses to be weak for our salvation.

Paul Tournier speaks of the cross in Christ's experience as the proof of God through failure: 'After the miracles in Galilee there comes the solitude of the cross. After the proof of God by success, there comes the proof of God in failure; a paradoxical proof, but how much greater, in fact, and more absolute, despite its apparently relative character.'[4] Tournier is here underlining the need for the witness of the Spirit in order to sustain growth and development of faith. However, he wants to understand the times of power as relative, and the weakness of the cross as absolute, to this witness. He is saying that it is not good for us to build up our sense of worth and faith from our experiences of power because these are only occasional moments upon our journey. John the Baptist, for example was in a moment plucked from the place of popular acclaim to find himself confined to the darkness of prison, assailed by doubts. He had boldly proclaimed, before any others could recognise his presence amongst them, 'Behold the lamb of God'; yet his last recorded words were of doubt and failing hope: 'Are you he who is to come, or should we look for another?' (Matt. 11.2–3). We have already noted that many of the early Christians who were channels of extraordinary power, nevertheless died in weakness and poverty. So we must fasten our faith not on the day of Pentecost, but on the fact of the cross. Yet before we explore Jesus's experience of failure at Calvary, we must also hold true to that aspect of the cross that does speak of its victory and power.

F.W. Boreham, a nineteenth-century evangelical and contemplative writer, spoke of the cross as being rather like a domino. The winner of the game is the one who puts his last piece down first. The cross is the last piece which God has laid down in his plan of salvation. The resurrection does not add to the event of Calvary, or make it any more effective, it witnesses to its efficacy and completeness! Therefore when Jesus shouts out, 'It is finished!' he is marking the fact that the last step in accomplishing man's salvation has been completed. The cross, with all its sense of abandonment and pain, also marks a way forward. For Jesus, as well as for us, the cross is not the end of the story. It has become the ultimate focus through which we see God's love in Christ. It tells us that the pathway for us to take if we too would be holy, is through the door of Calvary. The writer to the Hebrews has this very point in mind when he writes, 'And so Jesus also suffered outside the city gate to make the people holy through his own blood. Let us, then, go to him outside the camp, bearing the disgrace he bore' (Heb. 13.12–13). David Conner likens this holiness to a sort of stripping down where we come, like Jesus, to the place of true reliance on God which is the heart of what Jesus entered at Calvary. 'There is always the tendency to play at being spiritual, not least because the game is much more fun than the real business of facing the relentlessly nagging fact of failure which is that truth about myself. Yet to face the fact is to know dependence upon God.'[5] It is from this abandonment to God that we can move forward and through and with our sufferings, with grace, to places of power to proclaim and demonstrate, to times of patient endurance, to openness to carry our failures and brokenness, because what really matters is that God loves me and is with me within my experience.

Yet because the cross is the final piece for God to play, it is also the harbinger of the end, which is the fulfilling of the kingdom of God. Inextricably linked to Calvary is Pentecost; they cannot be separated, or cultivated for alternative styles of spirituality, one focused on brokenness and the other on power. No, we must not polarise what is essentially a whole experience. To seek the Spirit without the cross is to stalk the great events of success and power for their own sake, and that is idolatry; it is a mere seeking after self-satisfaction under the thin disguise of wanting to be 'Spirit-filled'. To take up the cross and all its apparent failure, but not to appreciate that it is God's final move in the plan of salvation and prepares the way for the coming of the Spirit, is to empty it of its power and leave no room for growing through failure.

The Spirit gathers all the moments of Calvary and with them ushers in the kingdom of God, and through them redeems the suffering of the faithful and the innocents. That is why the saints could rejoice in their sufferings, because these times became their Calvary and as such they pointed forward to the coming and the completing of the kingdom of God. The giving of the Spirit at Pentecost also tells us that God takes up and owns all the issues that were being resolved in Christ upon the cross. Nothing of his experience was lost, because it inevitably paved the way for the outpouring of Pentecostal power and blessing.

Pentecost also proclaims that there is real healing for all those who fail and suffer, even though such healing may have to wait until after death. The Holy Spirit is the Spirit of hope who will glorify all the moments of

Christ's life, including the losses sustained at the cross. Indeed, there will be times of great power when we shall overcome great odds, and there will be times when the same Spirit will bring us through a Calvary where we shall have no neat answers to explain our failures and losses. But through both experiences the Spirit reminds us of a better time when we shall share together in the fulfilling of God's kingdom and presence in fullness amongst us.

Maria Boulding draws together these two elements of power and powerlessness, showing that through them the cross becomes the vehicle for healing: 'If you have ever been sickened by the crumbling of some enterprise into which you had put all your best effort and love of your heart, you are caught up into the fellowship of Christ's death and resurrection . . . God has dealt with our failure by himself becoming a failure in Jesus Christ and so healing it from inside.'[6]

The cross is a place of brokenness as well as a place for picking up the broken pieces and moving on in the spiritual journey. The Japanese writer Kosuke Koyama tells us that the cross is not a bridge, for that is a symbol of transition from one side to another. It is rather an image of intersection where a number of roads meet. As such it gives a feeling of confrontation, encounter and conflict. It is a point at which people meet, and it stands for a painful solution.[7] The cross, then, offers us a unique failure, for it is one where hope meets despair, where the spirit of life embraces the taking of life. Out of its crushing embrace comes an openness to the future. If we are to gain something from the cross and our failures, we must first understand what it meant for Jesus. It is only from his experience of failure that we can learn to handle our own.

We shall now examine some of the moments of the cross which Jesus experienced. In doing this we are not undermining any of the importance of Calvary for salvation. However, aside from its theological significance, it was also an intensely human experience for Jesus who was in no way shielded from its impact by the fact of his divinity. If anything, Calvary was probably more painful for Jesus precisely because he was the Son of God. He had come in his incarnation from an eternity in unity within the Godhead. In stark and terrible contrast he is suddenly and personally subjected to a new experience, one of rejection and disowning. As John writes, 'He came to that which was his own, but his own (people) did not receive him.' (John 1.11)[8] This was never more so for Jesus than in his encounter with the cross.

The Scream

> Jesus cried out in a loud voice, 'My God, my God, why have you forsaken me?' (Matt. 27.46NIV)

> And when Jesus cried out again in a loud voice, he gave up his spirit. (Matt. 27.50NIV)

Here is Jesus, the Christ, in weakness asking questions and sharing his feelings minutes before his death. Only Matthew links the last cry with the agonising question which Jesus had asked previously. Judging from the word he uses, the Gospel writer seems to be focusing on the feelings and thoughts which were torturing Jesus' mind and heart. He uses the word '*kradzo*' which generally refers to inarticulate cries from fear or pain.[9] This is not to deny, of course, that faith was also present at these moments, because Matthew goes on to say that Jesus 'gave up his spirit', which implies a laying down rather than a taking of his life. However, in our desire to witness to the faith and triumph of Jesus in adversity, we sometimes overlook the emotional struggle that was going on.

The most obvious point about Jesus' outcry is that he received no answer to his question. There was only the sound of his emotional dereliction. Not even the hostile onlookers understood his cry. They thought that he was calling for Elijah to return, which was popularly thought to be the signal for the return of the Messiah. In other words, they thought his pain was pushing him into hysteria, and they tried to ease his lot with the sponge soaked in a mixture of wine and vinegar. But the question was genuine enough, and needed to be asked because Jesus was experiencing the alienation of a sinful humanity cut off from the presence of God, something entirely new for him. The separation anxiety must have been immense and crippling. In his feelings of devastation he needed to know 'why?'. Has this not been the cry of all the saints and martyrs down through the years? The Psalmist writes of his pains and asks, 'Why, O Lord, do you stand afar off? Why do you hide yourself in times of trouble?' (Ps. 10.1) Like all the prophets in trouble, Habakkuk wants to know why God does not deliver him from his misery; 'How long, O Lord, must I call for help, but you do not listen? Or cry out to you, "Violence!" but you do not save? Why do you make me look at injustice? Why do you tolerate wrong?' (Hab. 1.1–2). Jesus's cry tells us once and for all that the question of suffering does exist because he asks it for himself.

This brings us to the whole point about the value of asking questions about suffering in the first place. Sheila Cassidy doubts whether such questions do have any real value:

It gets me nowhere, and I know when I'm beat . . . Suffering *is*, in the same way that life *is*. It is a fact; denying it or ignoring it will not make it go away. I do not know if it has a meaning. Deep in my heart I believe it has but I don't really know. But this I *do* know: more important than asking why, we should get in there, be alongside those who suffer. We must plunge in up to our necks in the icy water, the mud and the slurry to hold up the drowning child until he is rescued or dies in our arms. If he dies, so be it, and if we die with him, so be it also. Greater love hath no man, than he who lays down his life for his friend.[10]

Cassidy makes a powerful case for identification with the sufferer in whatever way is possible for the carer. In fact her earlier book, *Sharing the Darkness*, very graphically likens the carer to those who stood at the foot of Jesus' cross. They could not do anything in real terms to alleviate his sufferings, but they could at least be 'in touch' or alongside him as he suffered.[11] Simply being there they reduced his sense of aloneness and who knows, perhaps their watching and praying enabled him to come sooner to the point of letting go and giving up his spirit! While not wishing to disagree with her commitment to care come what may, it does seem to me that Cassidy is saying that there is only value in asking questions if we have satisfactory answers. Yet there is far more to asking questions than merely wanting the right answers.

Often the question is more concerned to get out into the open the feelings of the person in question. When Jesus asked his one and only question of his Father, it was at least putting on record that he felt rejected and that it was important that this was said and heard. William and Kristi Gaultiere are attracted by the idea that Jesus was free to work through his negative feelings, and this was particularly true at Golgotha.[12] It is often very true that we cannot make decisions in our life because our emotions block the way forward. Rather than trying to deny our feelings by an appeal to faith it is far healthier to bring our repressed feelings in the open and lay them before God. To know, as Jesus did, that we are heard and that our feelings are respected, often gives us the release and necessary perspective to move forward. Jesus knew that his Father always listened to him, but this was the most difficult test for him to face because his pain and distress were so powerfully present within him. So asking the question was his way of stating how he felt before being enabled to hand over his spirit to the same Father. Jesus was silent before the questions of his accusers at his trial, but on the cross he cried out for answers.

Because of this, Jesus is united with everyone who cries out or who asks such questions which receive no answer. He is with us to say that it is really all right to ask the question, and that it is safe to do so even if there is no answer today or any day. Jesus' scream on Calvary is a sharing of very painful feelings and encourages us to give our hurt feelings a voice too. This in itself can be the beginning of healing. All too often we bottle up our hurt anger or rage, fearing that to speak it out is to deny our faith in God.

Some time ago I was counselling a single woman who was trying to come to terms with her depression. She was a nurse and had been interviewed a number of times by her GP and had been taking some medication to stimulate her emotions a little. However, she continued to slide into her feelings of anxiety. We met together for a number of sessions which were characterised by quite long periods of silence. Often her responses, which came at the end of these silences, would be muted and vague. Once when I asked her how she related to her father she struggled for almost twenty minutes to say in response, 'All right.' Clearly there was much more not yet said, but I did not feel it proper to intrude into the matter in a directive way. One day I asked her to describe to me how it felt to go home as she did on one of her periodic visits. I invited her, if it helped, to start with a mental picture of walking up the garden path to the house and knocking on the door, and to continue from there with what felt appropriate. Again there followed the long and silent struggle and then slowly she began to cry. What began as a series of sighs soon developed into a rapid flow of tears and emotion, increasing in intensity and lasting for about twenty minutes or more.

Needless to say, I did not interrupt. Afterwards she began to share quite freely how she had been mistreated and made to feel unwanted at home. Being able to cry out had been refreshing for her, because it was giving a voice to all the undenied feelings she had acquired. Her cry was affirming to herself, and it freed her to confront her own hurt and to choose to go forward from there. It was by no means a pleasant experience, but it did prove to be a healing one.

And so the cross invites us to join Jesus in his cry and not to be discouraged if no answer comes. It is enough to have asked the question. Just as Jesus was trusted with silence and mystery, so are we. Yet the silence was not a testimony to the fact that God had abandoned him or that he was not present within the terrible torture of the cross. Jesus could ask the question precisely because he knew that his Father was present to listen whether there was an answer or not. We might be tempted to think that it was easier for Jesus to ask the question because he knew that the next chapter of his story was to be the resurrection. Yet in that place of separation surely Jesus himself may not have been able to be aware of anything else save how he felt at that moment. We do not see what is next in our story and so, rather than trying to squeeze in some answer that might ease the pain, we often have only the choice to believe that our cry has been heard because God is somehow present in our troubles, and that this is enough for now.

Paul Brand and Philip Yancey, in *In His Image*, refer to the experience of Elie Wiesel, a fifteen-year-old Jewish boy who endured unspeakable horrors at the Buna and Auschwitz concentration camps.

> His worst experience was witnessing a twelve-year-old boy savagely punished on the gallows. Wiesel said the boy had the face of a sad angel, innocent and beautiful, and so unlike the gaunt, disfigured faces of most of the prisoners. The boy didn't belong on the gallows, but there he was. The chairs were tipped over and his body fiercely jerked. He dangled limply from the ropes, longing to be dead, but still barely alive for another half-hour. From behind Wiesel, in the row of anguished spectators, a man cried out, 'Where is God? Where is he now?' Wiesel heard a voice within himself answering the man, 'Here he is; He is hanging here on this gallows.'[13]

Sadly, Wiesel took this experience as a demonstration of a God who was dead and impotent. His friend François Mauriac, who was a Christian, could only embrace Wiesel when he saw the dark horror of his life, revealed in his eyes, and weep for the many deaths he had endured. He could weep with him because he knew in his heart that because of the cross, God was there in Auschwitz, sharing the suffering too.[14]

Jesus not only cried out his question because he knew he was heard, he also surrendered his cry. There came a point when, having forced out his feelings of failure, he then made them into a gift to give his Father. Luke records that his next words were, 'Father, into your hands I give my spirit' (Luke 23.46). John has a proclamation of vision and faith: 'It is finished!' (John

19.30). Neither of these statements actually answers his question, or makes it easier on his feelings, but they do reflect that the time has now come for moving forward, even if it means going on into death. Jesus had finished what he had to say; and so he becomes the model for all of us who come to our moments of needing to let go now that we have given our feelings a proper voice. Once the cry had been shouted there was no grabbing back or holding on to the hurt. It was all to be surrendered. Neither did Jesus attempt to explain to those around him the meaning of his failure, because his cry was committed to a stronger hand: his powerlessness was surrendered to one more powerful still.

How often have we felt the need to explain our failures to others so that we do not lose our status or sense of well-being before them? Yet even as we try to tell our story we are conscious of how we are still not satisfied within. We feel that we do not convince, or receive the healing we had hoped from our sharing. The cross tells us that we are free to shout out our loud cries and then surrender the moment to God and begin to face a future. We must leave behind all further speculation about 'why'. Our scream has been heard, now we must surrender to hope and look for a tomorrow somewhere with God who will still be our Emmanuel.

Nakedness

And they crucified him. Dividing up his clothes, they cast lots to see what each would get. (Mark 15.24NIV)

Those who passed by hurled insults at him. (Mark 15.29NIV)

Jesus answered him, 'I tell you the truth, today you will be with me in paradise.' (Luke 23.43NIV)

For many, the Christ who hung naked on the cross looked a far cry from the King of the Jews. Like the fable of the emperor who paraded in public without his clothes, Jesus now became something of a joke, mocked and insulted, exposed to popular view as a fake. All the promise of Kingdom and glory had faded away, and the man with authority like no other was reduced to nothing more than a naked and battered criminal. The mob which had once praised him in procession had now turned cynical and angry; such is the ugliness of human nature when its heroes fail them. There has always been that desire to expose and strip the defeated in order to make their defeat complete.

> There is no loincloth to protect the modesty but a violent insistence on total nakedness so that vulnerability is maximised. Those who work with victims of torture speak of the deliberate perversion of the relationship of intimacy. It is no accident that people are stripped naked, that they are genitally abused, humiliated and raped, for this constitutes the greatest humiliation that one human being can inflict upon another.[15]

So Jesus becomes the common man in his nakedness. He was subjected to an act of dispossession; when he lost his clothes he lost the privacy of his person. Christ, captured upon the cross, enters the world of those who feel robbed and reduced by their failure in society. In this he identifies with all those who are stripped of their dignity and made less than they perceive themselves to be. Ernesto Cardenal's poem based on Psalm 22, captures the range of dispossessed lives which Jesus enters into because he comes naked to his cross:

Why hast thou forsaken me?

My God, my God, oh why hast thou forsaken me?
I am but the travesty of a man
despised of the people,
laughed unto scorn in every daily newspaper.
Their armoured cars encompass me,
their machine gunners have set their sights on me,
barbed wire besets me round.
From morning until evening
I must answer to my name;
they have tattooed me with a number.
They have photographed me
hedged about by an electrical fence.
My bones may all be told as on an X-ray screen.
They have taken my identity away from me.
They have led me naked to the gas chamber;
and they have parted my garments among them –
yea even down to my shoes.
I call out for morphia but no one hears;
I call out in the strait-jacket,
call out all night long in lunatic asylums –
in the ward for terminal cases,
in the isolation wing,
in the home for the aged.
Drenched in sweat, I suffer
in the psychiatric clinic, stifle
in the oxygen tent, and weep
in the police station,
   in the prison yard,
     in the torture chamber,
       in the orphanage;
I am contaminated by radioactivity
   and all men shun me lest it might contaminate them.

But my words shall be of thee before my brethren,
and I shall exalt thee before the congregation of our
people:
my hymns shall rise up in the midst of a multitude.
There will be a banquet set before those who are poor.
And there shall be a great feast among our people:
the new people, that is to be born.[16]

Being naked also means having nothing to give. It is
to be in the place of vulnerability with no place to hide.
Jesus would not even hide behind the anaesthesia of the
sponge with its wine and myrrh, and he would not
escape his nakedness in sleep. Unlike Jonah who tried to
sleep in the bowels of the boat in order to escape the call
of God on his life, and unlike king Hezekiah who turned
his face to the wall and tried to sleep off the awful reality
of his forthcoming death, Jesus stayed awake to his vulnerability. This was his choice for us, for in so doing he
identifies with all those who feel that their failure is
open to the critical eyes of others and who feel that
there is no escape from shame and embarrassment. It is
at times like these that we feel worthless and want to
hide or play games with ourselves and dodge the full
impact of what is really happening. We are hurt and
crushed and in danger of giving up our faith. Perhaps
we have been wounded by our enemies or, what is far
worse, by our friends, and we are left feeling we cannot
live with others knowing what has happened, and so
deny we are hurting. Eventually we become hard and
the mention of such things, even long after the event,
still leaves us feeling sore.

I was talking once with a friend who was a minister
about an experience which had caused him and his wife
a lot of pain. He was on the verge of giving up his
ministry altogether. It was the policy of the church
which he served to elect (or re-elect) its minister after

every five years. The moment had now come when his term of office was complete and he had stood for re-election for the post of pastor. What had made the whole thing upsetting was that both he and his wife had to sit silently through the actual discussions as the church leaders discussed his merits or otherwise. Harsh criticisms were made of his failure to bring in more new people to the church. After a heated debate the vote was taken. He was duly elected, but by a narrow margin of just two votes; even the results were made public. He said that he was left feeling that he had been stripped bare in front of everyone and had no space given him to defend or speak for himself.

Failure like this is hard to handle and the temptation is to hide it away and not mention its name. Yet we find that it leaks out at unpredictable times, and we shout and scream and protest that it is unfair what has happened to us. Or the power of our past failure or hurt is triggered by some present event and we are undone again. We are plunged into depression and robbed of our usual energy and will to live. The way of healing is to face up to our nakedness and cease to try to deny that we are vulnerable. I like this poem by Amy Wilson Carmichael which encourages us to stay open to our cross, and, like Jesus, despise its shame:

> From prayer that asks that I may be
> sheltered from winds that beat on Thee,
> from fearing when I should aspire,
> from faltering when I should climb higher,
> from silken self, O captain, free
> thy soldier who would follow Thee.
>
> From subtle love of softening things,
> from easy choices, weakenings,
> (not thus are spirits fortified,

not this way went the crucified)
from all that dims Thy Calvary,
O Lamb of God deliver me.

Give me the love that leads the way,
the faith that nothing can dismay,
the hope no disappointments tire,
the passion that will burn like fire,
let me not sink to be a clod:
make me Thy fuel, flame of God.[17]

Christ's nakedness is our call to openness. It is a call
to go on loving and hoping even though everything is
lost. The amazing thing about Jesus is that the more
vulnerable he became the more he went on loving. He
didn't put up defences to protect himself, he didn't
retreat into some kind of cosy mediocrity. On the cross
he loved and forgave his tormentors, and this didn't
make his nakedness any less bloody or painful. Yet it
does tell us that through Christ we too can move
through our nakedness and vulnerability. We begin to
see that the worth of our personhood and dignity lies
beyond mere externals of what others see, and so we
can afford to love and forgive. This does not come
cheaply or without pain. For Jesus it meant Calvary, for
us it will mean taking up the cross also.

Our failures, which leave us feeling exposed, are also
the times and places when God chooses to strip away
our pretences, our outer defences. This is not done
because he delights in embarrassing us or pulling us
apart; it is because we have become less than ourselves,
have lost our dependence upon him or need to take
another step in the journey of wholeness and healing.
When Jesus rebuked Peter at Caesarea Philippi (Matt.
16.23), and later when he predicted that Peter would
deny him, he was not exposing Peter in order to put him

down or crush his sense of worth before others; it was a confrontation which challenged Peter to be real and not play the game of bravado. Far from crippling him for ministry, such encounters enabled Peter to become the kind of open-hearted man God had called him to be, and to lead the emerging church with the maturity and stability which he needed. We cannot 'go in' for making ourselves more holy or saintly or broken, as if it were some commodity we can acquire if we work hard enough at it. No, it is God who calls us into the stripping down and building up, and he does this by first calling us to the cross where a naked Jesus opens himself for the healing of a battered world.

Dread, an unhallowed and horrible thing in itself, can become holy dread. The safe and proper way to encounter and overcome the dread within us is not to fit out an expedition to journey into the interior. Those who do enter their own 'darkest Africa' this way, are apt to lose themselves in the jungles. The Christian does not enter upon this, the hardest task of life, at the place and time of his own choosing. He waits for God. To know that he has a journey to make which will threaten his peace, overcome his resistance and disturb his demons cannot be learnt too early in adult life. But the purpose of the Christian journey is not prompted by an introverted curiosity. It is not the cult of a fuller personality. It is obedience to God. The Christian has no particular interest in the symbolic fauna of the dark valley, of the wilderness, or of the deep sea of the unconscious. He encounters them as he encounters the cross, in the course of a journey, the object of which is beyond all these things. He has to pass through them, or they pass through him, for they are now God's purgatives. The soul becomes cleaner and the clearer for having passed through them. To follow Christ, the Lamb of God, wherever he goes, is to be attacked by wolves. This is simply the nature of the case as it was for Jesus and as it will be for the Christian. To obey the living Truth when every fibre of one's nature protests is to enter a mental defile. All the more painful decisions of life involve our dying to at least one aspect of our mental defences.[18]

Finally, we need to see that out of his nakedness Jesus offers us everything. Paradoxical as it may seem, hanging naked before the world, Jesus promises paradise to the next man who sees his own nakedness and failure. Silent before his accusers, Jesus now speaks out, and when he does it is to make an offer of more to come. The thief had acknowledged, not only to Jesus but to the other thief who raged against his sentence, his own guilt and his need to be remembered by someone and not be forgotten. The naked Christ says to him, 'I tell you the truth, today you will be with me in paradise' (Luke 23.42–43NIV). Hope and despair meet each other at the cross. It is a reminder that we should not be too attached to the idea of succeeding in this world as we are journeying to a more permanent home in the paradise of God. This is not escapism, it is being aware that we should not become too preoccupied with ebbing success nor become enmeshed in failure or in worry about what others will think of us. Both are a cul-de-sac on earth, but Christ offers us paradise.

The third man hanging there also wanted paradise, but he wanted it cheaply. He wanted to get away from the cross in order to be saved. We must come to the cross if we will be saved. For Jesus and for the repentant thief, this meant death. So it is for us. There is no easy escape from our failure, we too must taste the deaths which the cross will bring us if we would see life to the full. This will mean risking being vulnerable, naked and wide open. It is messy and at times totally unmanageable. We may have to die to all kinds of cherished hopes, ministries and ambitions. But this stripping of our self-sufficiency will bring us into total dependence upon Jesus, who will support us and fulfil us because we have recognised our need of him. Our failures make us naked before God and others but this can really be the place where we can learn to let go of our own importance and grasp the realities of paradise, the all-importance of seeing clearly and knowing the presence of God who loves us.

Suffering

See what a transformation!
Those hands so active and powerful
Now are tied, alone and fainting,
You see where your work ends.
But you are confident still, and gladly commit
what is rightful into a stronger hand,
and say that you are contented.
You were free for a moment of bliss,
then you yielded your freedom
into the hand of God
that he might perfect it in glory.

Death

Come now, highest of feasts
on the way to freedom eternal,
Death, strike off the fetters,
break down the walls that oppress us,
Our bedazzled soul and ephemeral body,
that we might see at last the sight
which here was not vouchsafed us.[19]

Powerlessness

Those who passed by hurled insults at him, saying, 'You who are going to destroy the temple and build it in three days, save yourself! Come down from the cross if you are the Son of God!' (Matt. 27.39–40NIV)

The chief priests, the teachers of the law and the elders mocked him: 'He saved others, but he can't save himself! He's the King of the Jews, let him come down from the cross.' (Matt. 27.41–42NIV)

Everything that was hurled as abuse at Jesus was actually true. He was the Son of God, at his death the temple curtain was torn signifying that the new temple of the human heart had been opened to the saving presence of God. He was the King of the Jews and he could save others. The only thing he could not do was save himself. Though they mocked him, Jesus never took seriously the invitation to come down and save himself even though there were angels present to rescue him.[20] To do so would have been to make the cross of salvation of no effect and so Jesus embraced powerlessness. However, his enemies did not see this embracing. What they saw was a failure. They saw someone who made great claims for himself now in weakness and shown up to be powerless to make good those claims. Yes, they had witnessed his healings, they knew about the raising of Lazarus. But now it seems that his power both to heal and do miracles and also the power of his popularity had faded away. They felt safe to come out in the open with their feelings of envy and hatred for this unnerving carpenter and rabbi from Nazareth. And so they pounced with their words of abuse and ridicule.

Yet Jesus refused to be drawn into a battle for power, he did not reply at all to their taunts. He embraced powerlessness in silence, he gave no word of explanation. Yet here, in this place of weakness, is revealed God at his best for us. Not in the demonstration of powerful acts but in love poured out in weakness for our salvation.

By embracing powerlessness, Jesus shares the common lot of all those who have had their abilities stripped away from them. He identifies with those toppled from power in coups and plots; those robbed of their natural functions through accident, old age or disease; those who are made refugees because others have stolen their homes; those who are marginalised, placed on the fringe of society because they are considered to have the wrong colour of skin, or the wrong sex or the wrong kind of body because it doesn't work properly like everyone else's.

The powerlessness of Christ also speaks to us about our experience or desire for the powers of the world to come. Our encounter with such power is not an escape, or an alternative to the weakness of the cross, it leads to the cross just as it did for Jesus. As his ministry of healing and restoration gathered momentum in some towns, so did the opposition. Pentecostal power inevitably brought him to the cross. That is why Jesus did not use his power to play safe or just stay in the places where his power was wanted and applauded. David Prior reflects upon the fact that our experience of power will remain small if we attempt to stay on safe, comfortable terrain. 'When Jesus moved out in the power of the Spirit, he was led to places and people where oppression, blindness, bondage and poverty reigned.'[21] For Christ was more concerned to be obedient to his Father than to hold on to power. So many of us in renewal long for power and wonder what has gone wrong when we enter weakness and powerlessness, and we long to regain our former glory. Michael Ramsey, in a sermon preached in Australia spoke of this relationship between power and fear: 'The human race is afraid and its fears are about power – about having it or not having it. Those who have it are frightened that they may be going to lose it. Those who do not have it are frightened of those with it.'[22] Now power is in fact what Jesus does offer us through our experience of the Holy Spirit. His resurrection words to his disciples on the day of his ascension were 'You shall receive power after the Holy Spirit has come upon you' (Acts 1.8). But it is interesting to note the context of these words. His disciples had been asking about power which would rule the nations, and Jesus talked about power to be witnesses to him. This dynamic power of the Holy Spirit would take them down the same trail as Jesus, to the cross.

Very often our sense of losing power is an opportunity to find ourselves. Some years ago when I was an assistant curate in Bolton I was approached by one of my parishioners and asked if I would go with her and pray for one of her granddaughters who was terminally ill with leukemia. I agreed to do this and together we drove to Nottingham where this seven-year-old girl lived. She was very poorly and lay in her father's arms as I gently laid hands upon her and prayed that God in his mercy would heal her of this disease and restore her to wholeness of life and limb. A couple of months later the girl died.

I was very sorry, but being far removed from the family was able to resume my duties without too much disturbance. Just over a year later the same woman came to me again and said that this time the older sister of the girl who had died was now seriously ill with the same disease. Immediately I was confronted with my feelings of being utterly powerless to help. I attempted to make excuses for why I would not be free to go with her to Nottingham again but I knew that I was lying. So

I admitted to Jean that I felt a failure, that I didn't feel qualified to pray for her other granddaughter because my prayers had proved so ineffective last time. I found it painful to consider the prospect of going down to Nottingham and facing another death on 'my' hands. Jean replied by saying that the family had appreciated that when I came the previous time I had made them no rash promises of healing and that I had come as a friend. At the time it did not do a great deal to console my mixed up feelings, but I did go and pray for Jean's other granddaughter. The second prayer was much the same as the first, I am sure, only this child began to get better and in due course fully recovered.

I do not understand why one child was healed and the other died. But there was a change in me and in my approach to power. I learned that more happened when I shared my weakness with Jean and her family. We were brought closer together in our fellowship and I was set free from the belief that my worth or status in ministry had something to do with the measure of power I could offer. I also learned that my access to power was completely in the hands of God and that there was nothing I could do to gain more from his hands. I just had to simply trust and obey and be obedient to God in whatever place of ministry he put me. This felt quite liberating because it also showed me just how much I was in the power of other people's opinions of me. Alexander Solzhenitsyn relates a similar feeling of freedom in *The Gulag Archipelago*. As long as he was trying to maintain some power in his prison, whether it was over food, clothing or health, he felt at the mercy of his captors because he perceived that they had power to determine how he felt about any of these issues. It was only when he realised and accepted, and even embraced his powerlessness, that he became free. The power of his captors over him had ceased. Paradoxically, he now became the powerful and they the powerless.[23] So Jesus, in powerlessness, shows us among other things a way to be free from spiritual competitiveness and to extend the availability of God's forgiving love to others. Our failure to be powerful may well be a blessing in disguise.

As a final thought about this element of failure and powerlessness on the cross, we must look at the cross's power to save and deliver. When Paul was writing to the Corinthian church he talked about the foolishness of the cross as well as the power of God (1 Cor. 1.18). It is from this bondage to the desire to be powerful that Christ in powerlessness sets us free. Ultimately, behind this quest for power are the demonic forces which hold humankind in bondage. Paul describes the death of Christ as a powerful act by which the principalities and powers are disarmed (Col. 2.15). A weakened and dying Jesus dethrones demonic powers from their tyranny over the affairs of men. This explains again why Jesus was so uncompromising about setting his face towards the cross; he would not be turned aside for anyone and denounced those who tried to prevent him. 'The reason why the cross is a victory is that it has opened a breach, once for all, in the prison wall of the selfish will to power. From henceforth and forever it shall be clear that only those who refuse to hold on to life (power) for themselves can enable others to live.'[24]

Darkness

It was now about the sixth hour, and darkness came over the whole land until the ninth hour, for the sun stopped shining . . . Jesus called out with a loud voice, 'Father into your hands I commit my spirit.' (Luke 23.44–46NIV)

Jesus hangs in the dark as he comes to the end of his journey. Exhausted and thirsty he dies. In a curious way he is both the centre of attention and at the same time lost from view. The darkness separates him even from the few friends who were there for him. Darkness seems to underline the feelings of isolation and loneliness that all of us feel when we have failed. There seems to be no room any more for comfort or support. It is from the dark that Jesus makes his exit from this world. There is no shining light, no band of angels accompanying him; he dies almost hidden from view.

Jesus has completed his journey from transfiguration to torture; from mountain top radiance to darkness on Calvary. Contrast the difference between Jesus, who could let go his mountain-top moment of glory, and Peter, who tried so hard to hold on to the glory and only let go when the darkness of the cloud hid it all from view. Just as the transfiguration experience was the day of the Lord, so is the darkness the day of the Lord, and Jesus can equally let go in the dark. In fact some of the Old Testament prophets spoke of the messianic age in terms of darkness rather than as the expected day of conquest over enemies:

'In that day,' declares the Sovereign Lord, 'I will make the sun go down at noon and darken the earth in broad daylight . . . I will make that time like mourning for an only son and the end of it like a bitter day.' (Amos 8.9–10NIV)

'The great day of the Lord is near – near and coming quickly . . . That day will be . . . a day of darkness and gloom, a day of clouds and blackness. (Zeph. 1.14–15NIV)

The Israelites glibly assumed that the day of the Lord would be their day, when God would rout and destroy their enemies. However, the prophets pointed out that the day of the Lord would be uncomfortable for the faithful and unfaithful alike. This is because it will be a day for God and not for man. On that coming day it is the name of the Lord which is to be vindicated and exalted and not the cause of the people. The darkness blocks our view of all but God because he is also Lord of the darkness.

Not many, if any at all, can enter our darkness with us. This is the private part of failure which none can see or share except God alone. We may brood and cry alone, or wallow in guilt. There often comes a point when our sense of worthlessness is too great to carry before others, so we retreat into the shadows; we abide alone. This is often the most powerful time as well as the most dangerous. It is in this place of separation from others that we make decisions about what to do next. The darkness that descends upon us can rob us of our vision of the future and so we turn in upon ourselves. There is no failure like lonely failure. It is most important for us to know that Jesus has been down this road before us, and likewise came all alone to the darkness. His life was the grain of wheat which for a long, dark moment was abiding alone, but then it was turned over to the Father to be broken for others: for the first and only time in his life, Jesus learned to die.

For all of us there will come those days when we are broken by certain events and feel alone and in the dark about why things seem to have gone wrong. That is the moment to share the darkness with Jesus and learn to hand over to God the moment and all its emotions, whether it eases the pain or not. If we hold on to our hurt it will crush us; if we give it to the Father we shall at least know that we have shared our feelings with one who knows us:

> Come ill, or well, the cross, the crown,
> The rainbow or the thunder –

I fling my soul and body down
For God to plough them under.

Robert Louis Stevenson

In his day of darkness and shadows, Jesus knew this and so committed his spirit to the Father. This was a supreme act of trust, because he knew there was a future beyond his death. We must not be tempted to hurry in at this point and plunder the cross and rob it of its importance with some form of easy triumphalism. There is always the danger in popular evangelical theology, while wishing to underline the accomplished work of Christ upon the cross and its victory, to paint a Christ who is controlling the events of the cross. The darkness tells us that this was plainly not the case. Here Jesus is tasting the bitter defeat of all those who are robbed of significance and thrown into the darkness, who are not wanted any more and so are discarded. Jesus felt such pain and isolation, first for himself and then for those for whom he was suffering. To those who watched, his death seemed such a waste, so ignominious and futile an end for what had held such great promise. All the disciples felt this – the women who came to anoint his body at burial, the men who had gone back to their former interests, all testified that they were sure it was all over. They continued to meet in the upper room, more out of a sense of loyalty and faded curiosity than in certain faith that he would soon turn up, alive. Yet the cross, with all its dark moments, is a real victory over the world, the flesh and the Devil, precisely because it is the place where all our failures are fully embraced and redeemed. I do not know how this is actually worked out, but I believe it is because Jesus came back from his failure; he rose from the dead.

The cross, then, brings together all our failures but also points the way forward to the possibility of a salvation which will defeat our failure. And so the cross is a tree of shame but it is also the tree of life. It seems that two spiritualities meet here and complement one another; the contemplative and the charismatic; suffering and conquest. Our danger is that we take one without the other. If we chase just the charismatic, then we collapse when we meet with failed expectations, or we look for some scapegoat. Far too often we have loaded others with accusations of lack of faith and belief, when all the while God is challenging us with failure. For those who contemplate only the sufferings of the cross, there is a need to embrace the Spirit of renewal who makes real the resurrection and widens our horizons to dare to hope and to see God in action amongst us. Calvary contains statements about failure and expectancy, and we need to hold both in balance if we are to handle our defeats with as much faith as we do our victories. The cross, with all its dimensions of our failures, calls us to empty ourselves, not that we might be less than who we are but that we might be filled with God. 'Have this mind among yourselves, which is yours in Christ Jesus, who . . . emptied himself . . . and became obedient unto death even death on a cross' (Phil. 2.5–8rsv)

> Two trees
> proclaim in spring
> a word to a world.
>
> One exploding
> into blossom
> trumpets glory.

One stretching
dead limbs
holds the empty
body of God.

Both speak
with due reserve
into the listening
ear of the world.[25]

6 GAINING FROM LOSING

'He is no fool who gives
what he cannot keep
to gain what he cannot lose.'

Jim Elliot, missionary and martyr

Throughout this book we have been examining some of
the Christian responses to failure, especially those
which have trivialised the experience by refusing to
engage the pain, rage or loss of the individual and focusing rather on the claim that this is in fact some kind of
secret success. An example of this is the remark I have
heard from many parents when they have lost their first
child through a miscarriage. They have been told not to
mind because most mothers lose their first pregnancy,
and there will no doubt be other children who will be
born into the family. Then they may be told, 'Your
child must have been very special and that is probably
why God decided to take him/her straight to heaven to
be with him.' But surely, we are to mind! A life has been
lost, a real person has died, and there must needs be
grief. The implications of the phrase 'never mind' or 'I
know it hurts but look at the blessings you have gained'
are often a disowning of the failure itself and a rejection
of that experience. I fully agree that we must not become so focused on our particular failure that we lose
sight of the grace and provision of God, but, as we have
seen, Calvary's cross tells us that failure itself is part of
the spirituality of following Christ the King. Yet surely
there must be some lessons that we learn from our
failures which add to our personal growth and holiness,

so that we can say we have gained something of real benefit from our failure?

It is often when the very things we have taken for granted are taken from us, like health and the ability to look after ourself, that in the process of crumbling that follows we undergo a transformation of character. This is no better illustrated than in the life of Jacob.

Even before he was born, Jacob was trying to get his own way. The Genesis record tells us that he was grabbing at the heel of his elder brother Esau in order to have pre-eminence over him (Gen. 25.23–26). That is how he got his name, Jacob, which literally means 'supplanter' but which could easily be translated 'twister' or to use a more modern idiom, 'con-man'. The battle at birth becomes the battle for birthright when Jacob tries to steal Esau's privileges of being the firstborn. This is consolidated when Jacob dresses up as Esau to fool his blind father into giving him the prophetic promises of primogeniture. The price for his arrogant ambition is exile as he flees to escape the wrath of his elder brother.

Yet despite his overwhelming need to succeed over others, Jacob's schemes always seem to end in failure. He arrives at his uncle Laban's house and agrees to serve him for the joy of marrying Rachel but is fooled into marrying the older and plainer-looking Leah (29.17–30). So he slaves for another seven years before marrying the woman he really loves. However, the plotting heart is never still in Jacob and he devises a way of enlarging his own herds at the expense of his uncle's, and once again Jacob is a man on the run as he is found out.

Finally, Jacob discovers that he cannot go home after all these years as his brother Esau is coming out to meet him with an escort of four hundred horsemen! Another scheme is devised and Jacob sends ahead of him presents of cattle and even his large family in the hope of appeasing Esau's twenty-year-old anger. Yet Jacob learns that, nothing deterred, Esau is still advancing with a veritable army. And so Jacob has run out of schemes and is at his wits' end. It is at this moment that God comes to Jacob in the form of an angel and a tremendous wrestling of wills takes place. Jacob realises, for the first time in his life perhaps, that he cannot win and sees his need of God's blessings and cries out for them (32.22–26). Yet before God does this he asks Jacob his name – an invitation to own and confess his inner nature cleanly before a holy God. This Jacob does; he confesses to being a schemer. So God blesses him but in renaming him Israel, the name with power and God, he is crippled (32.25–28). So in his weakness, Jacob actually has more power and influence than he has ever had in his life before. All his failures have brought him to confession and blessing and as a consequence he ceases to be a supplanter and becomes an intercessor who now asks blessings on behalf of others.

The apostle Paul testified to the same experience, that when he was weak he found new strength in God (2 Cor. 12.9–10). This was not some technique he had discovered whereby he found a way of increasing his experience of power, and so rejoiced to be weak and looked forward to being persecuted. He had in fact discovered the solidarity that God especially offers to the weak and marginalised, if only they have eyes to see it. Those who fail and those who suffer are offered a share in the grace of Christ, who has gone before all in his journey to the cross and the crown. This is the power in which Paul boasts, the power of grace to bring Jesus into our failures, to show us a way to live with a conquering faith despite all the losses.

This latter point is taken up by David Lim when he calls for Christians to become practitioners of what he calls 'cross-ethics'. He writes that a cross-ethicist is one who needs patience, who though broken by poverty and failure needs to be open to the freedom of the Spirit which comes from a right perspective of the cross.[1] Such a way of learning from the events of the cross offers us a unique energy to perform tasks beyond our previous ability and experience. It is essentially a freedom to hope, born out of suffering. Lim shows that this is not just fanciful dreaming, by referring to the resurrection. 'It proves that the ethics of the cross is not a foolish code of conduct of a visionary fanatic. Good Friday and Easter demonstrate that God intends to restore humanity and the world to wholeness ... Humans are being made whole and righteous; God is at work in the world creating peace and justice.'[2] Anyone who watched the news concerning the attempted coup in the Soviet Union during the three momentous days in August 1991 would perhaps have seen very much the presence of God in averting the attempt to reverse the course of *perestroika* and send the republics back into the dark ages of the Cold War.

Before we examine some of the 'gains' we do need to acknowledge that many who experience failure do not come out of it with a greater degree of wholeness or maturity. They emerge scarred and broken, and sometimes quite bitter that God should allow them to fail and suffer so. We must resist the temptation to defend God, or ourselves, from their criticisms by doling out shallow references to the hidden blessings that they will inevitably discover which will have made their suffering have some purpose; or to accuse them of not having enough faith by which they should have triumphed and come out of their failure with some new insight which makes the experience worthwhile. There is no easy way to respond to such deep sadnesses resulting from failure. We need to cultivate the spirit of Jesus who, when he was accused by Mary and Martha of not caring enough to prevent the death of their brother Lazarus, simply listened to their bitter complaint and wept with them.

Even if we are not able to see any gains from our losses we can at least acknowledge that after the pain and the rage have been voiced we still need to decide what we are going to do next. The day will come when we shall need to let go of our bitterness or cynicism and begin to live again. Jennifer Rees Larcombe discovered that one of the routes out of the trap of bitterness is learning to forgive God. In other words, choosing to let go of what we have been holding against God for allowing us to fail.[3] This is not to say that God is necessarily responsible for our failures but that, being sovereign Lord, he chooses to take the responsibility for the losses we have in life. The act of forgiveness is therefore an opportunity to own to our hurt feelings, to bring them out into the open and then to release them and be released from them. For many, this is the only way they can begin to go forward with their lives.

Many years ago I invited Jenny, my next door neighbour and a single parent, to attend a Christian musical called *Come Together*. During the evening there was an opportunity for people to receive prayer for personal growth and healing. As we drove home later, I asked Jenny if she had responded to the invitation to receive some form of ministry. She said that she had joined a group which was praying for people who had been hurt by divorce. During the course of the prayers she was suddenly challenged about her reluctance and inability to commit herself to marry her boyfriend. She said she had been sharply made aware of the fact that she was holding a lot of bitterness against God and herself for what had happened in the breakdown of her marriage. She had been physically abused by her former husband, and her struggling faith had been crushed by it all.

However, in the time of prayer she had made the choice to forgive God, to let go of holding bitter feelings against him. She said that she now knew that she could forgive herself; she had been plagued with thoughts that she had somehow contributed towards the violent nature of her husband and had always felt guilty. Now she felt forgiven and freed, and she did go on to marry her boyfriend and also recovered her faith and began to grow again as a Christian.

Another way forward from being entrapped by the pain of failure, to which Valerie Lesniak has drawn attention, is that it must be transmuted into compassion if it is to be of service in our lives.[4] She goes on to say that this is only possible within the assurance of acceptance that God understands. When Mother Teresa of Calcutta was asked by the writer Malcolm Muggeridge how she felt when the people she was trying to help died of malnutrition and disease, she replied by saying that because God has access to all our dark places then she could at least enable people to die with dignity. All failures, whether real or imaginary, says Gerard Hughes, are to be seen as opportunities for growth and knowledge of the truth that God, and God alone, is our rock, our refuge and our strength.[5]

Ron Smith, a Reader in the Church of England, lay dying in Bolton General Hospital. He was not very old and always bubbled with energy and vision in his desire to encourage people to be filled with the Holy Spirit and to know God's power in their lives. Now he was feeble and fighting for breath. As curate in the church in which he served I had got to know Ron and his wife Margaret very well; together we stood at his bedside holding his hands and praying with him. He looked at me and perhaps read the question in my mind as to why God would allow such a man to die when he still had so much to give. And so he told me that I mustn't forget what is written in Romans 8.37–39 and to make sure it was read out at his funeral.

> No, in all these things we are more than conquerors through him who loved us. For I am convinced that neither death nor life, neither angels nor demons, neither the present nor the future, nor any powers, neither height nor depth, nor anything else in all creation, will be able to separate us from the love of God that is in Christ Jesus our Lord (NIV).

Ron knew that he would have no solution to the mystery and the mess of his illness, but he also knew that he could not be separated from divine love. It was this knowledge that enabled him to let go, and which gave Margaret faith to face the future without him.

Having looked at some responses to those failures which cannot be explained or which do not have any apparent purpose, we must now turn to those times when our failures do come to us as a gift. Michael Apichella suggests that there are four basic reasons why God allows us to fail;

> As a means of bringing about a greater good.
> Failure keeps us from becoming too puffed up.
> Failure is due to unconfessed or volitional sin.
> Failure is sometimes due to bad decisions or natural disasters.[6]

As a Means for Greater Good

I am sure that most of us can think of moments in our lives when something that seemed to have gone wrong turned out to be a doorway to a better opportunity. This is not to deny, of course, that at the time our failure may have cost us dear and hurt very much. For some years I had a job which involved putting safety film on windows in order to make them shatter resistant. I loved this job, I had a partner who was a Christian and together we drove around the country working at a variety of places ranging from oil refineries to the penthouse suites of top company executives. Incidentally, I had managed to get jobs with the company for at least six other Christians who were all out of work.

Then suddenly, in 1975 when the government introduced the three-day working week, many of us were made redundant. I was furious and hurt, not the least because I really loved the freedom and the open road which the job gave me. Others who had started working with the company at a later time than me were kept on, and so I also felt victimised. Yet looking back now, I see that if I had stayed in that job I would have remained deaf to the call of God upon my life to the ministry, which had been continuously present in my life since I had been converted. Consequently, when I realised this, I did in fact go back to the works office and apologise for my bitter attitude and even explained what God had shown me through all these events.

This is what Evelyn Christenson calls the 'so-that' principle.[7] Basing her thoughts on Romans 8.28 she says that God has not removed every loss or hurt, but he has chosen to work through them and turn each one into a gain. Although her terminology is sometimes slick (e.g. 'God is in the business of turning your losses into gains'), she is concerned to point out that these gains are not necessarily sweeping successes. The gains she has in mind are, simply put, to 'gain the purposes of God'.[8] She quotes the words of Jesus: 'If anyone would come after me, he must deny himself and take up his cross and follow me. For whoever wants to save his life will lose it, but whoever loses his life for me will find it' (Matt. 16.24–25NIV). The gain in mind here is that of knowing Christ and following him. To quote David Lim again:

> Cross-ethics calls for participation with him who had nowhere to lay his head. Following Jesus who had no money, demands 'voluntary poverty' from his disciples: to lay aside those cherished attachments which cannot be carried on the way of the Cross. It calls for the abandoning of the pseudo-security of one's possessions in order to identify with the poor and follow Jesus unconditionally.[9]

It would hardly be conducive on the basis of this insight to call following Christ and taking up the cross some kind of success culled from failure. The gains to which God calls us can be bloody and messy, but they do form part of Christ's kingdom presence amongst us. Other examples quoted by Christenson, taken from the life of the apostle Paul, are the gain of proclaiming the Gospel despite the privations of suffering and imprisonment (Phil. 1.12f.); the gain of a growing and thriving church despite the set-backs and hardships of witnessing (1 Thess. 1.6–7); the gain of the grace of God despite continuous wrestling with personal weaknesses (2 Cor. 12.9).

To Keep Us From Becoming Puffed Up

Joseph, son of Jacob, was a gifted but pampered son. Jacob, who had to some degree been dominated by the favouritism of his mother Rebekah, unfortunately repeated the process of parental bias in the life of his second youngest son. Consequently even though Joseph was given dreams from God as a prophetic insight to the future, he none the less prided himself on his abilities and insights. Needless to say, his brothers

110

hated him for it and it was this which drove them to plot Joseph's downfall. Therefore Joseph was catapulted from favouritism to slavery in Egypt (Gen. 37).

However, in slavery Joseph had still not lost his gift of understanding dreams and he was of service to a number of people, eventually including Pharaoh himself. Yet there was a different spirit about Joseph as he worked now not with his own dreams but with those of others. Far from priding himself on his ability with dreams, Joseph was anxious to point out that his was a gift which belonged rightly to God. His failure in times of promise had humbled him, and in later days his humility was to prove the salvation of his own clan and people.

There is a lot in Scripture which points out that humility is the vantage point from which we are to see and understand the purposes of God in our lives and nation. Interestingly enough the word used here is 'ani', which means 'to be afflicted' and so the issues of failure and revelation are brought together. So the Psalmist can exult and say, 'My soul will boast in the Lord; let the afflicted hear and be glad' (Ps. 34.2)[10]

Another, and rather stark, example of this use of failure is that of the life of King Nebuchadnezzar whose story is told in the book of Daniel. He too had experienced some startling dreams which were also prophetical. The focus of the dreams was the transitory nature of kingly power and its dangers in contrast with the eternal power of the living God. However, in contrast to Pharaoh, this king defied the message of God and refused to acknowledge his need of divine guidance and support for his position. In an overnight attack of madness the great king was reduced to scraping the ground of the fields for his food; he became a dishevelled beggar. His sanity was only restored when he confessed his pride and so was brought to exalting and praising God who is all wise and powerful (Dan. 4).

111

There are many who can thank God for their failures because they were the very means of bringing them back from pride and teaching them true humility. Unfortunately it seems more likely that we will learn humility from what we lose than from what we gain.

The Result of Unconfessed, Volitional Sin

One of the most obvious examples of this from Scripture is Joshua's failure to conquer a relatively obscure town called Ai after his spectacular destruction of the city-fortress of Jericho. When Joshua came before God in brokenness and prayer to enquire why God had let them fail, he was told by Yahweh that there was sin in the camp because someone had stolen loot from the victory over Jericho (Josh. 7.7–12).

This account teaches us that there are times when God will not allow our sins to go unconfessed if we are to know his blessings among us. The failure at Ai is not overcome until it is pointed out that the guilty party is Aachan, and punishment is given. We need to be aware that this is an example of corporate responsibility familiar to the emerging life of Israel, but that with the development of scriptural revelation, it is rather the individual who is shown to suffer for his own sins. However, one of the lessons to learn from this story is that our sins do affect the lives of others, and can drag them into the failures which are properly our own doing. Consider for example the resultant effects of David's adultery with Bathsheba. The wider outcome of this sordid episode is not only the engineered death of Uriah, Bathsheba's husband, but the destruction of David's family as his other sons become threatened by their new brother Solomon. One by one the other sons rebel and are all killed.

God does not allow us to fail because he enjoys punishing us, but because he wills to discipline us and to bring us to acknowledgement of our sins and then restoration to holiness of life. Our failures then point us to the place of repentance. This was brought home to me very forcibly in the earlier days of my Christian life. During the mid-1960s I was a member of a Christian Union in a polytechnic. It was brought to my attention as chairman that one of the men had been molesting a girl. It was my uncomfortable duty to confront Ray and discipline him. We met together in a church to discuss the whole thing and it was a very difficult time indeed. When I asked him for his response he said that it was none of my business what he did, and anyway, he did not feel that he had done wrong and that Christians should be a bit more liberal in their attitudes. He was a very forceful and persuasive person and for a time I felt quite unable to argue the need for some form of discipline.

Quite suddenly I was given a prophecy by the Holy Spirit and after some hesitation I gave it to him. It was basically that unless he repented of his sins to God then the Lord would severely discipline him and bring all of his work to an immediate end. He laughed at these words, and said that they were just scare tactics on my part. However, we learned some days later that Ray had been admitted to the psychiatric wing of the local hospital suffering from a nervous breakdown. As a matter of fact he was still in the same hospital eighteen months later when I happened to be visiting there. He asked me to sit down with him beside his bed and he began to say that he knew that he was being punished for his arrogance towards God. Here he confessed his sins to God as we prayed together. Shortly afterwards he was discharged and returned home and later began attending his local church again.

I fully admit that this may well be an exceptional case, at least let's hope so, but it illustrates the point that God will not overlook our sins even if we try to do so, and he will often use failure to bring our sins to our proper attention.

Bad Decisions or Natural Disasters

This kind of failure is perhaps almost the easiest to accept because in a sense it does not involve God directly. When we have made bad decisions we see that we have only ourselves to hold responsible; when natural disasters happen we accept that it is part of the risk of living. This is not to say that we do not question God. Sometimes we wish that he would have prevented us from making mistakes, but this is really both an abdication of our responsibilities and reducing God to the role of puppet-maker. We also wonder why God does not prevent earthquakes and floods. Apart from questioning the wisdom of some who live in high risk areas this whole issue is almost impossible to understand. However, there are some bad decisions we make which are actually the result of misinformation we have chosen to believe.

In discovering what lies at the root of some of our failures, we go on a journey which is rather like a difficult birth which has to be fought over if the new life is to be properly received and established. Whatever stands in the way of giving birth to this new life has to be struggled with and sometimes discarded or cut away. As a counsellor I often meet people who feel that they can never please God, or that their prayer life is a continuous failure. In the process of listening it very often transpires that the reason behind their alleged failure is that they have some false conception of God, based perhaps on models of parenthood they have grown up with. Consider this example:

One woman kept trying harder and harder to please God but still felt inadequate. Her distorted God Image came out in a dream in which she pictured God as a magician in black evening dress. He was doing magic tricks and constantly bowing to applause from spectators. He had a dog, cat and rabbit that were trained to jump through a hoop when he called their names, which were Moses, Isaac and Jacob. In her dream, this woman felt like she was fourth in line. God would call her name and she would have to jump through a hoop for him. As a child she could never say her prayers properly enough for her father, so in her dream she could not jump through God's hoops properly.[11]

Before concluding this chapter let us outline some of the gifts which failure offers to us, whether or not we can discern any purpose to our experience. None of these may bring us the healing we may want from our failure, but they do help us to let go of the dead end to which our failures bring us, and help us to hold on to a God who promises to be the same tomorrow.

The Power of Helplessness

The following prayer was found on a piece of paper beside the body of a child at Ravensbruck concentration camp:

O Lord,
remember not only the men and women of goodwill,
but those of ill will.
But do not remember all the suffering
they have inflicted upon us;
remember the fruits we have brought
thanks to this suffering –

our comradeship, our loyalty, our humility,
our courage, our generosity,
the greatness of heart
which has grown out of all this;
and when they come to judgement,
let all the fruits which we have borne
be their forgiveness.

'Human helplessness is the crucible out of which victory could rise.' So wrote Catherine Marshall after rebuilding her life following the tragic death of her husband Peter when he was only forty-seven years of age.[12] She felt totally inadequate to manage her life and that of her baby son. However, her sense of insufficiency led her to the 'inexhaustible efficiency of God'[13] Finding God's availability in a time of failure she described as the power of helplessness.

Such times of crisis do bring us to the end of ourselves and to the greater possibility of dependence upon God. For many, caught up or seduced by their sense of power and competence, this is a spirituality which needs to be rediscovered and re-owned. The doctrines of success and inevitability lead us to the sense of our self-sufficiency, and this is nothing short of idolatry. In direct contrast to this are the words of Jesus, 'Without me you can do nothing' (John 15.5). Dr Arthur Gossip, some years ago now, described these as the most hopeful words in Scripture, 'For it is on the basis of the frank recognition of our utter fecklessness apart from him, that Christ enters into covenant with us and gives us His tremendous promises.'[14]

We can still find good news when we are weak, for God is for us also. For some, this recognition can only come with failure. Helplessness brings us to brokenness and to a greater openness to spiritual direction. It is here that growth is truly possible.

116

Accept surprises
that upset your plans,
shatter your dreams,
give a completely
different turn
to your day,
and – who knows? –
to your life.
It is not chance.
Leave the Father free
himself to weave
the pattern of your days.[15]

Watchman Nee, a Chinese Christian pastor, was imprisoned for his faith during the aftermath of the Communist revolution in his country. He had been a popular speaker and now he was silenced and deprived of fellowship. His sermons and talks were subsequently put together and a series of books released which became world-wide best sellers. One of these books is called *Release of the Spirit*. In it he wrote of the ways in which he felt that God was teaching him inner brokenness through his sufferings and failures, in order that out of this brokenness the release of God's Holy Spirit would become more pronounced. He also learned that this release of God's Spirit would not be to promote his own cause and prestige, but only that of Jesus and the Kingdom of God.

There are times when God comes to us in our failures to bring brokenness because we have not learned to decrease so that the presence of Christ may increase. It was John the Baptist who first uttered these particular words (John 3.30) and his brokenness took him out of the limelight and to prison and death. Yet his willingness to be broken opened up the pathway for Jesus and his disciples to really go forward in their ministry. Our failures and brokenness, if received by dependence upon God, will open up a way for God to use for others also.

The sacrifice acceptable to God is a broken spirit;
a broken and a contrite heart, O God you will not despise.

(Ps. 51.17)

Something else that we can learn from our helplessness is confession and forgiveness. Confession is not only a recognition and acceptance of our failure, it is also an awareness that we can go free. It means that we do not have to live under judgement. Confession means that our failure can be acceptable to God. Maria Boulding speaks of the Spirit of God having to batter through our proud defences in order to awaken in us the need for forgiveness. This is what is called the work of contrition whereby the bruised heart is set free for its lover.[16] We are once again on the road to recovery and wholeness as forgiveness brings us back to needing God's love. It is this truth which Mother Basilea Schlink expounds in her book, *Repentance – The Joy-Filled Life*. She underlines that it is as we repent that the kingdom of God is at hand for us, and this is the ultimate joy of living with God.[17]

This approach to repentance lies at the heart of penance in the Roman Catholic rite. Here, it is a commitment to work and grow from accepting and surrendering our failures back to God. What is more, as Christians we have to live in the open with our failure. So penance has become a shared experience with the emergence from the Lent season as the church's celebration of failure into the light of the Easter rising that is about to come. It is a time to learn anew the joys of sins forgiven as the church recognises it is on a journey from brokenness to wholeness through Christ.

If the ground is well dug by troubles, persecutions, detractions and infirmities – they are few who ascend so high without this – if it be well broken up by great detachment from all self-interest, it will drink in so much water that it can hardly be parched again . . . Tears gain everything, and one drop of water attracts another.[18]

Charles Colson, the former White House aide to President Nixon, said on television that it was through the failure of the Watergate scandal (for which he was partly responsible) and his imprisonment that he began to experience God's presence and love in his life. His time in jail offered him an opportunity to reflect upon the direction of his life and to see that it was his seeming self-sufficiency which had proved his own undoing. The failure of his plots and skills had ultimately brought him to salvation and to a relationship with God. He had learned the most important truth in life – that God wants a relationship with us. As such this takes priority over any useful service we may think we can offer God. I always think it is important to emphasise that in Jesus' last recorded words regarding the coming of the Holy Spirit he said that as a result his disciples would 'be' witnesses to him (Acts 1.8). I am sure that he is emphasising the quality of their living like Christ, rather than the quantity of power they were going to receive. This is also underlined by the words in Mark's version of the calling of the twelve. 'He appointed twelve – designating them apostles – that they might be with him and that he might send them out to preach and to have authority to drive out demons' (Mark 3.14–15). We might easily focus on the power encounters with demons, but the first reason stated is that these men might 'be' with Jesus. God is far more interested in what he can do 'in' us than just 'through' us.

> My goal is God himself,
> not joy, nor peace,
> nor even blessing,
> but Himself, my God;
> 'Tis thine to lead me there –
> not mine, but His –
> At any cost, dear Lord,
> by any road.
>
> *F. Brook*

So many people are so busy trying to be a success for God and others that they forget this high calling. Failure is used by God to bring us back to basics. We discover, if we are open, the need to recover our first love. Our fallen limitations lead us back to the Lordship of Jesus. Very often it is this displacement of the self for God that restores the spiritual balance in our lives.

Getting a Better Perspective

I asked God for strength that I might achieve,
I was made weak, that I might learn humbly to obey.
I asked for health, that I might do greater things,
I was given infirmity, that I might do better things.
I asked for riches, that I might be happy,
I was given poverty, that I might be wise.
I asked for power that I might have the praise of men,
I was given weakness, that I might feel the need of God.
I asked for all things that I might enjoy life,
I was given life that I might enjoy all things.
I got nothing that I asked for –
but everything I hoped for.
Almost, despite myself, my

120

unspoken prayers were answered.
I among all men,
most richly blessed.[19]

There was a very interesting statement of Joseph's
when he finally confronted his brothers from his
strength as Prime Minister of Egypt: 'You intended to
harm me, but God intended it for good, to accomplish
what is now being done, the saving of many lives' (Gen.
50.20NIV). They had plotted to get rid of him but God
used Joseph's failure to secure a future for his family. So
now, years later, Joseph had a better perspective of why
God had allowed so much pain to come into his life and
that of his father Jacob.

Our failures may well break our hopes, but they also
leave us no option sometimes but to trust God, that he
will give us in due course, a new perspective on the
event. This may, as with Joseph, take a lifetime.

Christian experience confirms that we can only come
to know the risen Christ when we have undergone
some kind of death, some disillusionment with ourselves and others, some loss or bereavement, some
sense of fear, hopelessness or meaninglessness and
have not tried to anaesthetise ourselves against it.
The answer is in the pain, which is revealing to us our
poverty and our need of God.[20]

7 JOB AND HIS FRIENDS:
A Case History of Ministry Failure

'I used to think that negative feelings were a sign of
failure which I must overcome or at least ignore . . .
Now I realise how wrong I was, for God is the God of
surprises who, in the darkness and tears of things,
breaks down our false images and securities. This in-
breaking can feel to us like disintegration, but it is the
disintegration of the ear of wheat: if it does not die to
bring new life, it shrivels away on its own.' *Gerard
Hughes*[1]

Without doubt the book of Job stands as one of the
great literary products of the world. Robert Watson has
described it as the first great poem of the soul.[2] Here
the issues of sorrow, change, pain and death are given
perhaps the most thorough treatment in the Old Testament. The sufferer wrestles with his feelings of terror
and weakness and also with the demand for the meaning of life. Job is not an example of silent and serene
patience! His endurance is characterised by screams, by
depression, by strong disagreements with his friends
and God alike, and by an almost violent determination
to live, despite his awful sufferings.

Job is presented to us as an emir living amongst the
settled inhabitants of the East, probably those of the
North Arabian Desert. He has seven sons and three
daughters, he possesses much wealth in the form of
sheep, camels, oxen and donkeys. He worships God
and leads an upright life. Job maintains a pastoral watch
over his children especially after their regular times of
feasting, just in case they may have inadvertently cursed

God during their celebrations and drinking. Naturally his riches meant power, and Job would be venerated not only for his wealth and power but also for what they signified, the constant favour of heaven. He would sit in the gate of judgement and like a judge offer advice for other people's problems. Job's life would be envied – until the day the bottom fell out of his world, when his possessions and finally his health were taken from him.

The writer of this book has obviously arranged his material very carefully in order to present the reader with the drama of unexplained suffering. The opening two chapters, written in prose, inform the reader of the battle in heaven which accounts for the unexplained calamities which overtake Job and his family. Then follows a series of intense debates between Job and each of his friends as they all seek to come to terms with what has happened and explain why. The whole focus of the book fixes upon the fact that, despite the advice and insights given by the friends, Job disagrees with their diagnosis, and as a result the discussions degenerate into argument and condemnation as the friends become more and more heated in their attempts to persuade Job to agree with them.

While the book is indeed an attempt to understand suffering it also provides deep psychological insights into how people respond to failure. First there is Job's failure, the reason for which is initially a mystery to his friends; later they are quite sure it is due to some undisclosed sins. Then there is the failure of the friends to convert Job to their viewpoint, and this is the main issue which the writer develops throughout the poetic section of the book. It becomes more and more apparent that the friends cannot face this failure, and they respond in varying degrees; they either accuse Job of rebellion or satisfy themselves that he is under the judgement of God and so nothing more can be said. The book closes the poetry section with a challenge from God to Job about true wisdom. The final chapter reveals Job repenting of his rash words and so God restores his life to health and prosperity. However, there is also a revealing insight into the characters in the story. God is angry with the friends because they have not spoken rightly about God, whereas Job has, despite all his strong feelings (42.7). So Job offers sacrifices once again and prays for his friends and they are forgiven.

This is a clue to the heart of the story; throughout the debate Job continually shares what is honestly upon his heart, but his friends seem more concerned to dole out dogmas than to try to enter into what Job is really suffering. Let us now examine this story in detail and observe some of the issues and lessons to be learned when our ministry is neither appropriate nor acceptable.

The Challenges in Heaven

The opening scene is in the courts of heaven and the 'sons of God' ('angels' NIV) are presenting themselves before God. Some commentators think that these are supernatural beings who had once been at strife with Yahweh, but who now, at stated times, pay enforced homage. The reason given for this is the presence of Satan, or the accuser, among them. However, it seems more likely that here we have angels worshipping and waiting upon God when an angelic being, the Satan, is given permission to approach.[3] The Satan is asked to consider the righteous life of Job who is renowned for his faithfulness to God. The accuser challenges God by saying that Job's faith rests entirely upon the fact that he has many possessions which God seems determined to protect. Should God deprive Job of his comforts, then there would be a change in his faith, and he would curse

God to his face. It seems that Satan is accusing Job of having a prosperity doctrine, but once his prosperity is removed his doctrines would disintegrate into anger and cursing. 'Have you not put a hedge around him and his household and everything he has? You have blessed the work of his hands, so that his flocks and herds are spread throughout the land. But stretch out your hand and strike everything he has, and he will surely curse you to your face.' (1. 10–11) God allows Satan to destroy Job's possessions as well as his entire family with the exception of his wife. However, he forbids Satan to actually harm Job himself. When next Satan appears before the heavenly throne, God points out that Job, though in pain over his losses, has nevertheless kept his integrity and so remained blameless in the sight of God. At the heart of his mourning, Job worships God and recites perhaps the classic response of faith: 'The Lord gave and the Lord has taken away; may the name of the Lord be praised.' (1.21NIV)

A second challenge is issued in heaven and is similarly engaged. This time Job is inflicted with painful sores which so scar his appearance that even his three old friends hardly recognise him when they come to comfort and support him. The one surviving member of his family, his wife, who is given one line of speech in the whole story, is exasperated by Job's apparent fidelity and urges him to give up holding on to his integrity and to curse God and die (2.9)! Yet in all his suffering Job does not accuse God of wrong, but meekly accepts the bad with the good. He remains sinless. However, the story is only just beginning for with the arrival of the three friends, Job's troubles become even more difficult to bear as his would-be counsellors make matters far worse for their former colleague.

Before proceeding to examine Job's experience and the conduct of the friends we need to address the question as to why God allowed Satan to attack Job in the first place. First we need to dispel the idea that what we have here is a dualistic contest in the heavens. It is not a case of two equals battling it out, with the human race as the pawns caught in the struggle. The Satan has to report to God his findings upon the earth and it is God who sits on the throne in heaven and who interrogates this spiritual adversary. Evelyn Christenson suggests that the testings and trials of Job are actually a compliment from God.[4] They speak of God's confidence in Job and in his ability to weather such tests. Unfortunately, Job does not benefit from this outlook, neither during his trials nor at the end when to some degree, 'God reveals all'. The more cynical of Christenson's readers may feel like saying, 'With friends like that, who needs enemies!' Yet does God need his confidence to be vindicated and proved to others in the first place? Surely the events on Calvary tell us amongst other things that God is not busily at work to defend his reputation and power. For there, he who claimed to be the son of God, was allowed to die in weakness, in the dark and with the sound of mockery and taunts in his ears.

It seems from the story that God is actually providing the Satan with a witness of faith under fire. Each time he seeks to destroy, Satan is served with a lesson in endurance, and is reminded that the purposes of God will ultimately prevail even through travail and suffering. Yet Job is unaware of what is taking place behind the scenes, and though the writer may be suggesting just such a connection between suffering on earth and spiritual warfare in heaven, the main focus of the book is on how each of the characters responds to and lives with unexplained failure.

Job's Complaining

After an initial period of quiet mourning in front of his

friends, Job begins to let out his feelings, and they come very strongly indeed. Far from a serene resting in his faith he begins by cursing the very day he was born (3.1–19). In the same speech he underlines the folly of receiving enlightenment if the person concerned lives in misery and cannot enjoy it. He sees death as a better alternative to such gifts, and even hints that God seems to be the one who hedges in the unfortunate to their fate. Job is basically asking the 'why?' question. Why had this calamity befallen him? He cries out to God from his pain, but there are seemingly no answers to his dilemma. Remember, his theological outlook was no doubt the same as his friends' at the beginning, but his experience of apparently undeserved disasters was to lead him to a different outlook. He believed that blessings were a sign of the favour of God and that sufferings were a mark of divine disfavour due to the unconfessed sins of the sufferer. As Job complains of his inability to cope with the unrelenting pain and his longing for a swift death to end it all he confesses, 'Do I have any power to help myself, now that success has been driven from me?' (6.13NIV).

Job goes on to challenge God himself, and demands that God shows him the charges set against him. In his confusion he begins to wonder if even God is against him, but he cannot quite bring himself to believe it. Job reminisces of the days when he enjoyed the favour of God and his family was all around him and he dwelt securely on his blessings and prestige (29.2–17). He underlines how he felt secure and convinced that he would die in such a comfortable place. He had come to take his good fortune for granted, but how quickly it had all been wrenched away. He had been toppled from his nest, and sooner or later this led him to question his relationship with God and his expectations of divine protection from the problems of life itself. Frank

Douglas sees this as a necessary learning experience for Job because he had come to rely upon his security and riches as a guarantee of God's blessing and had become stuck in his own personal development. While his questions were not necessarily answered, Job could never again take God's bounty for granted.[5] This is what Job is referring to in his final speech after God has spoken to him when he says, 'I have uttered what I did not understand . . . Therefore I despise myself, and repent in dust and ashes' (42.3,6). Jacques Ellul in his book *Money and Power* notes that Job is one of only three rich men in the Old Testament who is not condemned for his wealth and this is because it is quite clear from their stories that they came to love God and not their wealth.[6] Job's love for God was true, but it was deepened by what he lost and by what he questioned, for at the end of his screaming and raging he discovers that God is still there and he can do nothing else but go on loving him.

We must not fail to appreciate that the core of Job's speeches is his ability to verbalise his powerful feelings and questions and at the end of the day to lay it all at the feet of God in humility. However, his words and feelings have proved too strong for some to stomach. Joseph Parker, one of the greatest evangelical preachers during the latter part of the nineteenth century, argued that Job's speeches were full of profound mistakes and that they were only excusable because they were perpetrated by an unbalanced mind.[7] He went on to say that 'in our very frankness we should strive at least to speak in chastened tones and with the mystic spirit of hopefulness.'[8] In other words, Parker is saying that true spirituality doesn't share its feelings, especially its more passionate and strong ones. It is indeed this very quality which rouses the friends to declare what is acceptable behaviour and belief for the true believer. However,

Robert Watson sees a very different spirit in Job's cries of dereliction. He believes that the intensity with which Job longs for death is actually a sign and a measure of the strong life that throbs within him.[9] Yet what is for Job a protest for life, his friends misinterpret as a defiance of proper belief and conduct. It is this very inability to really see what is going on in front of their eyes which brings them to cause Job more pain and lay themselves open to the wrath of God.

So far we have looked at two kinds of failure: the failure of Satan to see faithfulness in man and the failure of Job to know the presence of God in his sufferings. Now we shall examine a third, the failure of the friends to counsel and minister to the needs of Job.

Job's Friends: Failing in Counsel

> To whom can any man say, 'Behold here I am. See me in my nakedness, my wounds, my secret grief, my despair, my betrayal, my pain. My tongue which cannot express my sorrow, my terror, my abandonment. Listen to me for a day, an hour, a moment. Lest I expire in my terrible wilderness, my lonely silence. O God! Is there no one to listen?' *Seneca*

There is no doubt that these friends arrived with the intention of helping Job out of his troubles. The shock of seeing his actual condition when they arrived rendered them virtually speechless. They adopted the routine of those repenting and mourning in order that God would forgive and heal. Who knows what was going through their minds; what deductions they were already making about why this had befallen their friend and confederate? However, they elected at first just to sit in silence beside him. According to the text they did not know what to say because of the magnitude of his sufferings (2.13). They adopted this stance for seven days.

This was probably the most constructive thing they could have done. Far too often we imagine that good counselling consists in the ability to give out good advice. Whatever the place of giving such guidance, it must be truly earthed in the ability to really listen to the other. This is because listening is communicating the fact that we truly value what the other has to say, and want to give him or her breathing space to speak it all out. There is an apocryphal story mentioned by Frank Lake in *Clinical Theology* concerning the famous German psychoanalyst Freida Fromm Reichmann who fled from Nazi Germany during the persecution of its Jewish citizens during the 1930s, and went to live in the United States. A rich businessman asked if he could come for an interview in order to have help and solve some of his inner problems. He was refused continuously until he offered a large remuneration for some limited time of therapy. He was eventually granted just one interview and was greatly helped. When in later years a friend heard of this story she asked the doctor why she would not see this businessman and was told in reply that when she first came to America she could not really speak English very well. 'But you did see him and he was marvellously helped. What did you do then?' The doctor replied, 'Well, every time he paused in his speech I said something like "uhumm" and so he then went on to say something more. Likewise when he paused I said "hmm" or "yes". The important thing however, was that he knew that I was listening to him and so he was enabled to get off his chest whatever was there!'

It was Henri Nouwen who said that listening was like giving another the hospitality of space where changes can begin to take place. We live in a world where people are starving not just for food but for the space to be heard. Also, the listening is at least three dimensional. I not only listen to the other but I also listen to God and to myself. In order to have the word of God for another I must be able to listen out to the voice of God and be enabled to receive his word for the other. This was in fact part of the learning for the Servant mentioned in the prophecies of Isaiah who was also a prophetic fore-runner of the Christ. Consider for example:

The sovereign Lord has given me an instructed tongue,
　　to know the word that sustains the weary.
He wakens me morning by morning,
　　wakens my ear to listen like one being taught.
The sovereign Lord has opened my ears,
　　and I have not been rebellious;
　　I have not drawn back.

(Isa. 50.4–5NIV)

The servant has God's word for the needy because he learns to listen to God for them. What a marvellous healing gift is this listening to offer to another![10] I am surprised, in this day of renewed emphasis upon the Holy Spirit and the charismatic gifts (amongst others), that in the desire to understand the word of knowledge and the word of wisdom there has not been reference to the Holy Spirit calling us into the quiet where we may learn to listen to God. Yet listening to God for another is not so easy as it may seem, precisely because we may have our own beliefs and agendas which get in the way of listening. We may be threatened by what the other person has to say, and feel that we must stop them speaking in order to tell them what we consider to be right or wrong. I am not implying that we sacrifice what we believe or surrender our morals but the important fact is that we must first satisfy ourselves that we have really listened with the ears of Christ before we can asume to speak the word of God. This is exactly where Job's friends failed in their ministry of counselling.

It is to their credit that the friends' solidarity of silence enabled Job to give voice to his feelings and bring them out into the open. This is often the value and power of a listening heart. It was Dame Cicely Saunders who said, 'If someone is in a climate of listening, they will say things they wouldn't have said before.' Beforehand Job had uttered his conviction of faith that God was in sovereign control of his affairs. He has not changed his beliefs, but now he is free to say what he is feeling because this part of his life is just as important as his faith. However, the friends are not heartened by Job's choosing to share his feelings but are horrified that one of their company should utter such words. They immediately take the offensive in order to bring Job into a 'proper' place of rest. What follows forms the real heart of the book; it is the consequence of ministry being rejected or receiving disagreement from Job. The friends begin all their speeches from assumed viewpoints and consider Job's refusal to agree with them as proof positive that they are right and he is wrong. Their replies to Job's speeches become more and more hardened as they are drawn into the battle to win the argument and triumph in their own viewpoint and soon lose sight altogether of the sufferings of their friend. Let us look briefly at each of the counsellors in turn.[11]

ELIPHAZ, THE ELDER STATESMAN

It is clear from his opening words that Eliphaz wants to save Job from as much pain as possible and give all the comfort he can. He reminds Job of the days when he was the counsellor offering help to others who suffered. Surely Job should not be unduly surprised that things have gone wrong in his life. Then Eliphaz gently encourages Job simply to confess his sins and lay them at

God's feet where he will find forgiveness and restoration.

Eliphaz seeks to establish the worth of his counsel by impressing upon Job his encounter with the supernatural – what in today's terms might be called a 'signs and wonders' ministry. He tells him that he has been given a word of knowledge during his sleep and that the spirit of God came upon him in anointing (4.12–16). In effect, Eliphaz is saying that his counselling advice is not from a human source but was supernaturally given. This reminds me so much of those who endorse their ministry to others with constant reference to how God had personally given them the advice and ministry they offer. Whilst not wishing to deny that the Holy Spirit does give insights and guidance, I can't help but feel that many such times it is a way of claiming an authority to speak which one has not been given. We use such words as a device to get our own agendas into the lives of those who come for help. We should weigh our words carefully, and not cheaply or lazily claim that they come from God.

Eliphaz also bases his ability to give direction upon the fact that he is a man of experience. One of his favourite expressions is 'I have seen' (cf. 4.8; 5.3,27; 15.17). Here he is pulling rank on Job in order to crush his viewpoint and bring it into line with his own. The tragedy, of course, is that Eliphaz's knowledge of God is not entirely spurious, but in speaking of his own beliefs he is no longer listening to Job and completely overlooks the fact that his friend stands before him in so much pain, and with his family life completely ruined. So often our ministries fail because they have never really started. We all too often see our primary objective as being to bring others into line with what we hold dear; with winning rather than loving. Questions become a threat, and like Eliphaz we hotly pursue the enquirer in order to bring them to a place of accepting what we say. As a means of persuading Job to be at peace, Eliphaz promises him prosperity upon conformity. He tells Job that God will protect him from all future calamities; there will be no famine in his lands and even the wild beasts will stear clear of his property. In other words, Eliphaz is prophesying what God will do for the repenting Job. But has he any right to say these things to his client?

Here prophecy is reduced to little more than a carrot to coax a recalcitrant client. The prophetic gift is not to be cheapened by casual promises of glory; it brings into disrepute the whole issue of charismatic gifts. When we examine the prophecy of Eliphaz we find that he is not describing the real world but some utopia of his own hoping. The Christian Church is littered with the shattered faith of those who have put their trust in the prophecies of others and made shipwreck of their hopes. Eliphaz is not in receipt of the word of God for Job, but is anxious to get his friend to repent and so move on in his life. Here is another source of failure in ministry, the fact that we start with the assumption of what is wrong and see 'our need' as moving the other through a procedure by which we feel they will arrive at our predetermined destination of blessing. This becomes paramount for the counsellor, who soon completely loses sight of any ability to be in touch with the client's pain and trauma.

Yet what courage and determination Job shows in refusing the offer to repent of things he honestly believes do not refer to him. He is not claiming to be sinless either; he is basically saying that his sins amount to the same as is common to all men and that therefore they do not explain why he is suffering so horrifically. It is interesting to note how the kindly Eliphaz responds to Job when the latter cannot take his advice. In his second speech he openly accuses Job of letting his sins run away with him; '. . . a man who is vile and corrupt, who drinks up evil like water' (15.16NIV). In his final speech he lists the sins that Job has committed in secret: 'You stripped men of their clothing, leaving them naked. You gave no water to the weary . . . you sent widows away empty-handed and broke the strength of the fatherless' (22.6–10NIV). Eliphaz has rapidly moved from gentility to outright accusation and condemnation. All because Job would not comply with his insights. He finds this too threatening, and so takes the offensive and in the process allows himself to become more concerned about his own ability to minister to this friend rather than with being of real help to a man in personal agony.

BILDAD, ADVOCATE OF SOVEREIGNTY
This man, though also concerned to see Job restored to blessing, is none the less more interested in making theological statements than in trying to understand what Job is going through. In two of his speeches he refuses outright to listen to what Job is saying (8.2; 18.2–4). He finds Job's words too hot to handle, and as far as he is concerned they seem to be an attack upon the justice of God. Therefore Bildad emphasises the sovereignty of God and the fact that mere man cannot question what the Almighty does. 'Domination and awe belong to God; he establishes order in the heights of heaven . . . If even the moon is not bright and the stars are not pure in his eyes, how much less man, who is but a maggot – a son of man who is only a worm' (25.1,5–6NIV).

It seems that Bildad feels that God's reputation is under fire and he must defend it. Like Eliphaz he appeals to the wisdom of tradition but gathers it together as a means to silence Job's outbursts (8.8–10). In other words he is telling Job that he has no right to his feelings and words and that he should simply submit to the wisdom of God and repent and receive restoration. Robert Watson comments that Job's words represent new ideas to Bildad who has no sympathy with them. He is a man for whom his own tradition and wisdom is paramount and for him this is the most important issue in Job's suffering.[12] Theodore Robinson sees Bildad undergoing a kind of metamorphosis as he listens to Job's outcries. He notes how people who are naturally kind and sympathetic can be stirred emotionally into opposition and almost into hatred by a shock to their feelings and a denial of their creed.[13] This is an all too common feature of our ministry. When those we seek to help inadvertently challenge our own beliefs by the honesty or forcefulness of their own sharing, we feel compelled to defend our own agendas. In doing so we lose sight of the very reason we are there, which is to help them. Consequently Bildad succumbs to the desire to succeed in presenting his case, and far from listening to Job actually goes on to the attack. He is soon carried away by his fears and, like Eliphaz, accuses Job and his family of sinning, as a result of which they are now suffering (8.4; 18.21). Bildad failed his friend because he hid behind his creeds and made himself deaf to Job's feelings. Joseph Parker remarks that the doctrine of God's righteousness and justice was perfectly orthodox but Bildad used it as a weapon to smite the prostrate patriarch. His principle was right but his application was very defective.[14] In contrast to this counsellor who regarded strong feelings as suspect evidence of a faulty faith, it is reassuring to know that the Saviour we love and adore is such a person who is 'able to touch the feelings of our infirmities, yet because he was tested in every way like ourselves, yet without sin. In the light of this, let us approach his graceful presence and obtain mercy and find the grace we need for our time of trial'

136

(Paraphrase of Heb. 4.15). It is no small wonder that the root word for Jesus/Joshua in the Old Testament means 'to be spacious'. God gives us space in Christ Jesus to tell out our souls and be heard. Knowing that we are heard brings us to the place where we can now listen to God and receive whatever help or discipline or healing may be necessary. There was no room for Job's hurting in Bildad's life. If we are going to be good carers of our fellow men then let us give ourselves to listening first, and not interrupt the process by an anxious need to protect our beliefs from others' doubts.

ZOPHAR, AN ANGRY COUNSELLOR

Zophar has no further insights to offer to the occasion, he merely repeats the well-worn statements of the other two would-be counsellors. Immediately his anger is spilling out and he wants to silence Job and rebuke him for his words. He takes what Job has said far too personally and automatically concludes that every word that Job has spoken demonstrates his sin and guilt. Zophar actually longs for Job to be judged so that the matter of his obvious sinfulness can be speedily dealt with. 'Oh, how I wish that God would speak, that he would open his lips against you and disclose to you the secrets of wisdom' (11.5–6NIV).

It is very clear that Zophar is disturbed by hearing Job, and yet instead of exploring this challenge he immediately concludes that Job is in fact rebuking him personally: 'My troubled thoughts prompt me to answer because I am greatly disturbed. I hear a rebuke that dishonours me . . .' (20.2–3NIV). He cannot stand back and be objective about what Job is feeling, he only hears his beliefs being attacked and concludes that this is an attack upon his person. This is not an uncommon response for a counsellor who may well feel that he has become the focus of the client's feelings and suddenly allows himself to be drawn in. In Zophar's case he goes on the attack because he is feeling rebuked. He also accuses Job of various sins such as oppressing the poor and seizing other people's property. Therefore Job is getting his just deserts. He goes on to give a graphic if all-too-enjoyable description of how God is punishing Job for his many wickednesses.

It is clear that Zophar has nothing to offer Job except accusations and the expectation of doom. This is because his own feelings have got entangled in his counselling and he is now defending his hurt emotions. It is often so true that when we step into the place of helping another, this very place we now stand in becomes very uncomfortable for us and exposes many of our own unresolved feelings. It is a very vulnerable, and yet creative, place to be, for it gives us the choice of discovering our own needs and finding healing, or of hiding them away because we are more concerned about looking right than being all right. Zophar chose the latter course and so failed to be of any help to his former friend. As we have already said, because of his basic dishonesty with himself his friendship melts away and his hostility for Job takes root in his heart.

ELIHU, INTOXICATED WITH HIS OWN IMPORTANCE

The fourth counsellor has not been mentioned in the book so far, which has led some commentators to conclude that his speeches are an addition to the original book. However, it could be equally true to say that the writer is deliberately creating a dramatic effect by suddenly introducing him at this point in the story. The three friends had run out of arguments and stood once again silently before Job, but this time with exasperation and anger rather than shock at what had happened to him. Elihu chooses this moment to launch himself into ministry. However, it soon becomes clear that he rather enjoys his role of having the last word. His speeches are threaded through with appeals to his own youth, and yet he follows them up very quickly by saying that he himself has as much (if not more) to offer Job. 'I am young in years . . . that is why I was fearful, not daring to tell you what I know . . . But . . . it is not only the old who are wise, not only the aged who understand what is right. Therefore I say: "Listen to me" ' (32.6–10NIV). Elihu in fact is very concerned that Job should listen to what he has to say, and repeats the injunction no less than seven times.[15] By using the occasion for an opportunity to get over his own viewpoint so firmly, he has ceased to be a counsellor and has become a preacher.

Elihu is over-anxious to have his say and impatient to get his words out: 'Must I wait, now that they are silent? . . . I too will have my say; I too will tell what I know. For I am full of words, and the spirit within me compels me; inside I am like bottled up wine . . . I must speak and find relief' (32.16–20NIV). He also feels the need to establish his spirituality and insights in order to gain respect and response from Job. Often he refers to his own humility and gifting by the spirit of God. He claims that the Spirit is compelling him to speak (32.18). He claims to be walking uprightly with God and that the spirit of God is upon him (33.4). Finally he claims to have revelations and prophetic insights which must be heeded: 'I get my knowledge from afar . . . be assured that my words are not false; one perfect in knowledge is with you' (36.3–4NIV).

Yet Elihu does not dispense any insightful revelations, nor does he go much further than his three friends. He homes in on the fact that, theologically speaking, man is unable to understand and therefore question the authority and management of God in the affairs of humankind. Therefore he rejects and condemns Job for his very questioning of God. He also betrays the judgementalism of his friends when he assumes that behind the scenes lie Job's wicked acts. He accuses Job of arrogance by claiming himself to be sinless (33.9), of wrongdoing (33.17), of keeping company with evildoers (34.8), abduction (36.20), and unbelief (43.9). So Job must repent of his sins and God will restore him to favour.

Elihu is the worst kind of counsellor. He demonstrates a false kind of humility which really prides itself on its so-called wisdom from on high. His counsel has to be taken wholeheartedly because it comes by revelation from God and there is no room for arguing with that! Upon reflection we can see that Elihu's appeal to the charismatic spirit upon him is but a device to avoid listening and sharing in Job's uncertainties about God. This is exactly the dilemma facing those in renewal who do not see the power and the protection of God in their lives. There is the temptation to appeal to special revelation to explain it all away. How often do we see Christians living under the burden of other people's expectations and insights? It is too often a crushing burden, and what is more it is stamped with an unreality not worthy of the name of Christ.

The other issue to mention, of course, is the need for some counsellors to be seen to be powerful, and this is reinforced when others take their directives on board. Job would not play this game with his counsellors, and despite his sometimes indiscreet words he sought long and hard to be true to himself and maintain his own integrity.

Conclusion

This story of Job which we have briefly examined could almost be subtitled 'How not to counsel'. The friends' failure in ministry was basically a breakdown in their ability to really listen to Job and not necessarily have any answers but to stay in touch with his pain. Job, in fact, stated that one of his greatest desires was that his friends would really hear what he was saying; 'Listen carefully to my words; let this be the consolation you give me' (21.2). Instead he found their words devastating, and as such they increased his despair: 'How long will you torment me and crush me with your words?' (19.2).

Another reason for their failure was that they assumed in advance that they knew why Job was suffering, and despite his protestations they stubbornly repeated their well-worn dogmas. Their counselling had one sole aim, to enable Job to respond to their assumptions about his need and the correct procedures to meet them. This made them inflexible in their approach, which in turn increasingly alienated Job from them. One of the reasons we fail in our caring is because we are not open to the person as a priority. This is not to suggest that we abandon our beliefs and become absorbed in the other person's outlook. But good counselling is about enabling the other to discover where they are, and the clarity that this brings will resource them to choose where to go from there in their journey with God.

Also, the friends could not take it when Job rejected their advice. They became locked into their own need to win or look right or be successful in their ministry, whatever the costs to the sufferer. If this is true for us then we need to acknowledge what is happening and be prepared to lose our need to win in the greater need to care for and love the other.

And what of Job himself? The story by no means paints him as a perfect example of saintliness, as is clearly shown by the denunciation of his friends and his open challenge to God to come and show him what horrendous sins he had committed to deserve such punishment from the Almighty. Indeed, when God speaks from the whirlwind, he challenges the fact that Job has uttered many words without knowledge, the very fault he has identified in his counsellors (38.2).

I suggest that the writer of the story is not primarily trying to solve the riddle of suffering, but amongst other things is saying that it cannot be satisfactorily solved. In other words there are some failures we will have to live with as best we can. This Job does with tenacity, humility and integrity. He holds on determinedly to the fact that he knows that he has not committed any sin to merit his misfortune: 'I will maintain my righteousness and never let go of it; my conscience will not reproach me as long as I live' (27.6). His humility is immediate however, when God reminds him of the limits of his knowledge: 'My ears have heard of you . . . and I repent in dust and ashes' (42.5–6). Job realises that although his questions will not be answered he has discovered one great truth, that God is with him; and that is what his heart has longed to know. God has listened to all of his words and has picked out the need behind the questions and fulfilled it. There are no explanations of the heavenly battle; the heart of the problem is to be assured of the presence of God.

T.H. Robinson suggests that in the Christian gospel we do have a further development in our attempts to grapple with the mystery of suffering and our failure to find an answer:

> The incarnation and the crucifixion, especially the latter, have shown us beyond dispute or doubt that suffering is not merely a human experience; it is also divine. When once we have seen in that tortured frame and heard in that last despairing cry of desola-

tion the very heart of God himself, we know we can take our stand on at least one firm spot. For if He whom we recognise as the universal Creator, the Lord of history, the Ruler of mankind, can endure pain beyond all man's imagination, then there must be a meaning in it. In that faith we may rest.[16]

In the words of Dietrich Bonhoeffer, 'The first service that one owes to others in fellowship consists in listening to His word, so the beginning of love for the brethren is learning to listen to them.'[17]

NOTES

Chapter 1   WINNERS AND LOSERS

1 Roger Woddis, 'The Loser's Song', published in *Radio Times* 1989.

2 John V. Taylor, *Enough is Enough* (SCM Press 1975).

3 ibid., p. 22.

4 Andrew Walker, *Enemy Territory* (Hodder & Stoughton 1987), p. 84.

5 Vance Packard, *The Status Seekers* (Penguin 1981) p. 173f.

6 Valerie Lesniak, 'The Myth of Success' *The Way* vol. 29, no. 2, April 1989.

7 Stuart Ewen, *All Consuming Images: The Politics of Style in Contemporary Culture* (1988) p. 70.

8 Robert Lifton, *The Broken Connection* (1979), quoted in the *San Francisco Chronicle* 18th September 1988.

9 Cheryl Forbes, *The Religion of Power* (MARC Europe 1986) p. 12.

10 Anthony Campolo, *The Power Delusion* (Victor Books 1986) p. 11.

11 Quoted from an interview in *Cornerstone Magazine* 23rd October 1980. See also Napoleon Hill, *Think and Grow Rich* for a fuller idea of the spiritist thoughts underlying his teachings.

12 Norman Vincent Peale, *The Power of Positive Thinking* (Fawcett Crest 1983) p. 52f.

13 Article entitled 'Suicide' in *Reader's Digest*.

14 Jeff South, 'Failure', used by permission.

Chapter 2   WE ARE ON THE WINNING SIDE

1 Kevin Springer (ed.) *Riding the Third Wave* (Marshall Pickering 1987).

2 William Temple, *Readings in St John's Gospel* (Macmillan 1943), commenting on John 16.8–11.

3 Thomas A. Smail, *The Giving Gift* (Hodder & Stoughton 1988) p. 190.

4 J.B. Phillips, *The New Testament in Modern English*, Romans 12.2.

5 Os Guiness, *The Grave-digger File* (Hodder & Stoughton 1983).

6 Luke 16.1–12; cf. Matt. 10.16; 1 John 2.15–17.

7 *Enemy Territory* p. 109.

8 John White, *Flirting with the World* (Hodder & Stoughton 1987) p. 68ff.

9 *Enemy Territory*, p. 133.

10 *Enough is Enough*, p. 87.

11 Richard Quebedeaux, *By What Authority?* quoted in Cheryl Forbes, *The Religion of Power*, p. 62.

12 Robert Schuller, *Living Positively One Day at a Time* (Fleming H. Revell 1981) p. 201.

13 Quoted in *Christianity Today* 5th October 1984, p. 12.

14 Douglas Frank, *Less than Conquerors* (Eerdmans 1986) pp. 201–227.

15 ibid., p. 227.

16 *The Works of John Wesley*, 3rd edn. (Peabody, Mass., Hendricksen 1972, reprint 1984) vol. 1, p. 188.

17 Henri Nouwen, *Gracias* (Harper & Row 1984) p. 62.

18 'The Myth of Success', p. 131.

19 David Prior, *Jesus and Power* (Hodder & Stoughton 1987) p. 16.

20 ibid., p. 20.

21 A.W. Tozer, quoted in Prior, *Jesus and Power*, p. 169.

22 *The Religion of Power*, p. 101.

23 *Jesus and Power*, p. 172.

Chapter 3   DOCTRINES OF DISTORTION

1 Florence Bulle, *God Wants You Rich and Other Enticing Doctrines* (Bethany House 1983) p. 9f.

2 ibid., p. 25.

3 *Jesus and Power*, p. 48.

4 Compare such Scriptures as Matt. 10.24–5, where the disciple is called to the Jesus lifestyle and suffering. Rom. 5.2–3 underlines how God's grace meets with our suffering in order to work godliness of character in our lives.

5 Richard J. Foster, *Money, Sex and Power* (Hodder & Stoughton 1985) p. 29. Compare also the words of the apostle Paul, who said, 'The love of money is the root of all evil' (1 Tim. 6.10).

6 Dr Lee Salk, quoted in Bernard Gavzer, 'What People Earn', *Parade Magazine* 10th June 1984, p. 4.

7 *Less than Conquerors*, p. 136.

8 A.W. Tozer, *I Talk Back to the Devil* (Harrisburg Christian Publications 1972) p. 30f.

9 Matt. 6.9ff., The Lord's Prayer; Eph. 6.18, for the saints in battle; Phil. 4.6–7, intercessory prayer with thanksgiving; cf. also Rom. 12.12; 1 Cor. 7.5; 1 Thess. 5.17.

10 Eph. 1.15–19; 3.14–19; Col. 1.3–6; Phil. 1.3–6.
11 Merlin C. Carothers, *Power in Praise* (Coverdale House 1974)
    p. 75.
12 *God Wants You Rich*, p. 46.
13 Evelyn Christenson, *Gaining Through Losing* (Scripture Press
    1983) p. 36.
14 *The Giving Gift*, p. 201.
15 Dietrich Bonhoeffer, *The Cost of Discipleship* (SCM 1959) p. 79.
16 Donald G. Bloesch, *Faith and its Counterfeits* (IVP Illinois 1981)
    p. 62.
17 Amy Wilson Carmichael, 'No Scar?' in *Toward Jerusalem* (SPCK
    1936, Triangle edition 1987) p. 85.

Chapter 4 SIGNS AND WONDERS AND FAILURES

 1 Bob Schwartz, BBC Radio 2, The Claire Rayner Programme,
    12th December 1990.
 2 Dermot Power, 'The Pain and Potential of Powerlessness', *The
    Way* vol. 29, no. 2, April 1989.
 3 *Less than Conquerors*, p. 107f.
 4 Maria Boulding, *Gateway to Hope* (Fount 1985) p. 37f.
 5 David Watson, *Fear No Evil* (Hodder & Stoughton 1984)
    p. 140f.
 6 For a fuller survey of the results of this kind of ministry you
    might like to read and compare the findings of the following two
    books: a) Wallace Benn and Mark Burkhill, *A Theological and
    Pastoral Critique of the Teachings of John Wimber* (Harold Wood
    Booklet no. 1, 1988) obtainable from The Administrator, St
    Peter's Church, 15 Athelstan Road, Harold Wood, Essex RH3
    OQB; b) David Lewis, *Healing: Fiction, Fantasy or Fact?* (Hod-
    der & Stoughton 1989).
 7 Brendan Byrne, 'Failure and New Testament Reflection', *The
    Way* vol. 29, no. 2, April 1989.
 8 Henri Nouwen, *In the Name of Jesus* (DLT 1989) p. 63.
 9 Central Television, *Friday Night Live* 8th February 1991.
10 Cf. e.g. Rom. 5.3; 8.17–18; 2 Tim. 3.12; Phil. 3.10.
11 *The Cost of Discipleship*, p. 81f.
12 Sheila Cassidy, *Sharing the Darkness* (DLT 1989) p. 59.
13 ibid., p. 64.

Chapter 5 CHRIST AND A CROSS FOR FAILURES

 1 Edward Shillito, 'Jesus of the Scars'.
 2 Sheila Cassidy, *Good Friday People* (DLT 1991) p. 2.
 3 Dom Dominic Gaisford, 'Cast your Bread upon the Waters' in
    Maria Boulding (ed.) *A Touch of God* (Triangle 1988) p. 173.

4 Paul Tournier, *The Person Reborn* (SCM 1977) p. 33.

5 David Conner, 'Holiness, Leadership and Failure', *The Way* vol. 29, no. 2, April 1989.

6 *Gateway to Hope*, p. 9.

7 Kosuke Koyama, *The Three Mile an Hour God* (SCM 1979), p. 42.

8 John 1.11 (the words in brackets are mine).

9 For a fuller discussion of this word consult W.E. Vine, *Expository Dictionary of New Testament Words* (Zondervan 1982) p. 259; or Thayer's *Greek-English Lexicon of the New Testament*, (Zondervan 1962).

10 *Good Friday People*, p. 114.

11 *Sharing the Darkness*, p. 60.

12 William and Kristi Gaultiere, *Mistaken Identity*, p. 151.

13 Paul Brand and Philip Yancey, *In His Image* (Zondervan 1984) p. 279f.

14 François Mauriac refers to this moment in the Foreword he wrote for Wiesel's autobiography, *Night*.

15 *Good Friday People*, p. 81.

16 Ernesto Cardenal, *Marilyn Monroe and other poems*, tr. Robert Pring-Mill (Search Press 1975) p. 79f.

17 Amy Wilson Carmichael, 'Make me thy Fuel' in *Toward Jerusalem* (Triangle 1987) p. 94.

18 Frank Lake, *Clinical Theology* (DLT 1966), p. 733f.

19 Dietrich Bonhoeffer, *The Way to Freedom* (Collins 1966) pp. 16, 19.

20 Matt. 26.53 records that Jesus said at his trial that he could, if he wanted, call on more than twelve legions of angels: 12,000 in all.

21 *Jesus and Power*, p. 68.

22 Michael Ramsey, sermon mentioned by George Appleton in *Hour of Glory* (DLT 1986), p. 72.

23 Richard Foster refers to this story in *Money, Sex and Power*, p. 205.

24 David Prior, *Jesus and Power*, p. 163.

25 Ralph Wright, 'Two Trees', in *Simpler Towards the Evening* (The Golden Quill Press, Francestown NH 1983) p. 64.

Chapter 6 GAINING FROM LOSING

1 David Lim, 'A Plea for an Ethics of the Cross', *Transformation* vol. 3 no. 4, Oct/Dec 1986, pp. 2–5.

2 ibid., p. 5.

3 Jennifer Rees Larcombe, 'Where Have You Gone, God?', *Renewal* July 1990, pp. 6ff.

4 'The Myth of Success', p. 137.
5 Gerard Hughes, *God of Surprises* (DLT 1985) p. 124.
6 Michael Apichella, *When Christians Fail* (Kingsway 1988) p. 12.
7 *Gaining Through Losing*, p. 7.
8 ibid., p. 19.
9 'A Plea for an Ethics of the Cross', p. 4.
10 Cf. also Deut. 8.2–3; Ps. 10.17; 69.2; Prov. 16.18–19; 29.23;
   Isa. 57.15.
11 Leigh C. Bishop, 'The Dream of the Magician; A Case of Para-
   taxic Distortion, *Journal of Psychology and Christianity* 4 (2) 1985,
   p. 12.
12 Catherine Marshall, *Beyond Ourselves* (Hodder & Stoughton
   1972) p. 153.
13 ibid., p. 155.
14 Arthur Gossip, The Interpreter's Bible (Thomas Nelson
   1953/4).
15 Dom Helder Camara, *A Thousand Reasons for Living* (DLT
   1981) p. 72.
16 *Gateway to Hope*, p. 110.
17 Basilea Schlink, *Repentance – The Joy-filled Life* (Marshall, Mor-
   gan & Scott 1969) p. 19f.
18 Teresa of Avila, *Living Water*, ed. Sister Mary ODC (DLT 1985)
   p. 24.
19 Anonymous Confederate soldier, American Civil War.
20 Gerard Hughes, *God of Surprises*, p. 134.

Chapter 7 JOB AND HIS FRIENDS: A CASE HISTORY OF MINISTRY
FAILURE

 1 *God of Surprises*, p. ix.
 2 Robert A. Watson, *The Expositor's Bible* (Hodder & Stoughton
   1892) p. 3.
 3 cf. 1 Kgs 22.1–28 and 2 Chron. 18.18–22; a lying spirit is to be
   found around the throne of God, etc.
 4 *Gaining Through Losing*, p. 36f.
 5 *Less than Conquerors*, p. 58f.
 6 Jacques Ellul, *Money and Power* (IVP 1984) p. 43.
 7 Joseph Parker, *The People's Bible* (Funk & Wagnell 1889) vol. 11
   p. 26.
 8 ibid., p. 76.
 9 *The Expositor's Bible*, p. 98.
10 An excellent book which gives insights into acquiring listening
   skills is Anne Long, *Listening* (DLT Daybreak 1991).
11 For a fuller summary of the friends I recommend the very interesting book by T.H. Robinson, *Job and His Friends* (SCM 1954).

12 *The Expositor's Bible*, p. 136.

13 *Job and His Friends*, p. 80.

14 *The People's Bible*, p. 58.

15 Elihu's command to Job to listen to his words are to be found in
   32.10; 33.1,31,33; 34.2,10; 36.2; 37.14.

16 *Job and His Friends*, p. 124.

17 Dietrich Bonhoeffer, *Life Together* (SCM 1954) p. 87.